NORMAN MAILER

In the same series:

S. Y. AGNON   *Harold Fisch*
SHERWOOD ANDERSON   *Welford Dunaway Taylor*
LEONID ANDREYEV   *Josephine M. Newcombe*
ISAAC BABEL   *R. W. Hallett*
SIMONE DE BEAUVOIR   *Robert Cottrell*
SAUL BELLOW   *Brigitte Scheer-Schäzler*
BERTOLT BRECHT   *Willy Haas*
ALBERT CAMUS   *Carol Petersen*
WILLA CATHER   *Dorothy Tuck McFarland*
JOHN CHEEVER   *Samuel T. Coale*
COLETTE   *Robert Cottrell*
JOSEPH CONRAD   *Martin Tucker*
JULIO CORTÁZAR   *Evelyn Picon Garfield*
JOHN DOS PASSOS   *George J. Becker*
THEODORE DREISER   *James Lundquist*
FRIEDRICH DÜRRENMATT   *Armin Arnold*
T. S. ELIOT   *Joachim Seyppel*
WILLIAM FAULKNER   *Joachim Seyppel*
FORD MADOX FORD   *Sondra J. Stang*
MAX FRISCH   *Carol Petersen*
ROBERT FROST   *Elaine Barry*
GABRIEL GARCÍA MÁRQUEZ   *George R. McMurray*
MAKSIM GORKI   *Gerhard Habermann*
GÜNTER GRASS   *Kurt Lothar Tank*
PETER HANDKE   *Nicholas Hern*
ERNEST HEMINGWAY   *Samuel Shaw*
HERMANN HESSE   *Franz Baumer*
CHESTER HIMES   *James Lundquist*
HUGO VON HOFMANNSTHAL   *Lowell W. Bangerter*
UWE JOHNSON   *Mark Boulby*
JAMES JOYCE   *Armin Arnold*
FRANZ KAFKA   *Franz Baumer*
SINCLAIR LEWIS   *James Lundquist*
GEORG LUKÁCS   *Ehrhard Bahr and Ruth Goldschmidt Kunzer*
NORMAN MAILER   *Philip H. Bufithis*
THOMAS MANN   *Arnold Bauer*
CARSON MCCULLERS   *Richard M. Cook*
ALBERTO MORAVIA   *Jane E. Cottrell*
VLADIMIR NABOKOV   *Donald E. Morton*
FLANNERY O'CONNOR   *Dorothy Tuck McFarland*
EUGENE O'NEILL   *Horst Frenz*
JOSÉ ORTEGA Y GASSET   *Franz Niedermayer*
GEORGE ORWELL   *Roberta Kalechofsky*
KATHERINE ANNE PORTER   *John Edward Hardy*
EZRA POUND   *Jeannette Lander*
    (*continued on page 148*)

MODERN LITERATURE MONOGRAPHS

GENERAL EDITOR: Lina Mainiero

NORMAN MAILER

Philip H. Bufithis

FREDERICK UNGAR PUBLISHING CO.
NEW YORK

Copyright © 1978 by Frederick Ungar Publishing Co., Inc.
Printed in the United States of America
Design by Anita Duncan

Library of Congress Cataloging in Publication Data

Bufithis, Philip H
  Norman Mailer.

  (Modern literature monographs)
  Bibliography: p.
  Includes index.
  1.   Mailer, Norman—Criticism and interpretation.
PS3525.A4152Z62   813'.5'4   74-78438
ISBN 0-8044-2097-1

For Linda
"That in black ink my love
may still shine bright."

Contents

Chronology

1923:   On January 31 Norman Mailer is born to Isaac Barnett and Fanny Schneider Mailer in Long Branch, New Jersey.

1927:   Family moves to Eastern Parkway, Brooklyn.

1939:   Graduates from Boys' High School in Brooklyn. September: enters Harvard to study aeronautical engineering.

1941:   Submits his first short story to Whit Burnett's *Story* magazine and wins first prize in the magazine's annual college contest.

1943:   Graduates from Harvard with honors (S.B. in Engineering Sciences).

1944:   March: marries Beatrice Silverman. Is inducted into the army and serves overseas for eighteen months.

1947:   September: completes the manuscript of *The Naked and the Dead* and departs for Europe, where he studies at the Sorbonne.

1948:   May 8: *The Naked and the Dead* is published. July: returns to the U.S. where he actively campaigns for the election of Henry Wallace, the Progressive Party's candidate for President.

1949:   Goes to Hollywood and works on an original screenplay, which Samuel Goldwyn rejects. Birth of first child, Susan.

1950:   Returns to the East.

1951:   Is divorced from Beatrice Silverman. *Barbary Shore* is published.

1953–63:   Is a contributing editor to *Dissent*.

1954:   Marries Adele Morales. Helps found *The Village Voice*.

1955:   *The Deer Park* is published after extensive re-writing.

1956:   Writes a weekly column for *The Village Voice* from January to May.

1957:   Birth of second child, Danielle. "The White Negro: Superficial Reflections on the Hipster" is published in *Dissent*.

1959:   *Advertisements for Myself* is published. Birth of third child, Elizabeth Anne.

1962–63:   Is divorced from Adele Morales. Marries Lady Jeanne Campbell. Birth of fourth child, Kate. *Deaths for the Ladies (and Other Disasters)* is published. Writes a monthly column for *Esquire*, "The Big Bite."

1963:   Is divorced from Lady Jeanne Campbell. Marries Beverly Bentley. *The Presidential Papers* is published.

1964:   Birth of fifth child, Michael Burks.

1965:   *An American Dream* is published.

1966:   *Cannibals and Christians* is published. Birth of sixth child, Stephen McLeod.

1967:   Mailer produces, directs, and performs in *Wild 90*, a film premiered on January 7. The dramatic adaptation of *The Deer Park* (starring Beverly Bentley, Rip Torn, and Hugh Marlowe) premieres on January 21 at the Theatre de Lys in New York and closes on May 21. *Why Are We in Vietnam?* is published. Part of the novel is produced as a one-act play (starring Beverly Bentley and Rip Torn) in Provincetown in the summer. Mailer participates in the October antiwar march on the Pentagon and is arrested. Is elected to the National Institute of Arts and Letters.

1968:   *The Armies of the Night* is published. His sec-
             ond film, *Beyond the Law*, is released. *Miami
             and the Siege of Chicago* is published.

1969:   Wins the National Book Award, the Pulitzer
             Prize, and the Polk award for *The Armies of
             the Night*. Runs unsuccessfully for mayor of
             New York. Covers the flight of Apollo 11 for
             Life.

1970:   Is separated from Beverly Bentley. *Of a Fire
             on the Moon* is published.

1971:   *The Prisoner of Sex* is published. His third film,
             Maidstone, is released. A reading performance
             of *D.J.*, a one-act play based on *Why Are We in
             Vietnam?*, is given in New York. Birth of
             seventh child, Maggie Alexander, to Carol
             Stevens.

1972:   *Existential Errands* and *St. George and the
             Godfather* are published.

1973:   *Marilyn* is published.

1974:   *Barbary Shore*, adapted and directed by Jack
             Gelber, premieres at the Public Theatre in New
             York on January 10 and closes on January 27.
             Signs a one-million-dollar contract with Little,
             Brown to write a multivolume novel.

1975:   *The Fight* is published.

1976:   *Genius and Lust* is published.

1

○○○

Biography

The conflict between the requirements of the self and the demands of society is a central issue of our time or any other. Norman Mailer has rendered this theme with more energy of style, more ideational power, and more vivid drama than any other American writer to emerge since World War II. His international reputation would seem to support such a claim. His books have been translated into more than twenty languages. They stir foreign audiences because, notes Anthony Burgess, they are "political, which is a great recommendation to all Europeans, and British fiction is just about un-exportable manners. I mean 'political,' of course, in the widest sense—the sense of protest or counter-protest."[1]

Although critical consensus regards Mailer as one of the two or three finest American writers of his generation, he presents a special problem to anyone trying to arrive at a clear understanding of his work for he has gained notoriety as a public figure as well as a writer. Indeed, his extraliterary activities—acts of civil disobedience, running for mayor of New York, four tempestuous marriages, contentious remarks on television talk shows, wild behavior at parties—have caused him in many quarters to be more read about than read. One might easily say that his public role has been a self-aggrandizing one, that since the publication of his fourth book, *Advertisements for Myself* in 1959, he has been huckstering himself into fame—and doing the job skillfully. This, in fact, is the favorite view of his detractors.

It is a view, however, predicated on the false assumption that his so-called public performances are strategies designed to promote his books. Actually, Mailer's escapades are crucial to the *creation* of his work, not to its *promotion*. He behaves as he does the better to write. By methods that he himself does not fully understand, for they are in large part subconsciously motivated, he tries to realize in his life the beliefs, hopes, and imaginings that he expresses in his work. He tries, in other words, to validate the ideas advanced in his books by eventfully acting them out in the world. "Till people see where their ideas lead, they know nothing," he has said.[2] As one would expect, the process becomes cyclical, for what Mailer discovers by testing his fictional ideas in the world is the need to modify or enlarge upon those ideas by writing more books. The important point is this: there exists in the case of Norman Mailer, more so than in the case of any other living American writer, a symbiotic relationship between life and art.

To *do* in one's life what one has *said* in one's art is as firm and successful an assertion of creative individuality as can be imagined. Any writer who can thus integrate life and art—the examples of Byron, Twain, Fitzgerald, and Hemingway come to mind— becomes a public figure. He becomes the embodiment of one's own private desires for self-actualization. He becomes, in short, a culture hero.

By involving himself in the major crises of our time, Mailer has endeavored to reanimate for modern man a belief in the struggle between God and the Devil. Man's courage—or lack of it—against the cancerous encroachments of technology, authoritarianism, and mass values will contribute, Mailer believes, to the outcome of that struggle. Mailer's engagements in national events represent his attempts to oppose such encroachments.

In 1948, at the age of twenty-six, he actively campaigned for Henry Wallace, the Progressive Party's candidate for President. He gave over twenty-five speeches as a member of the Progressive Citizens of America, wrote articles for the *New York Post*, and spoke on the subject of academic freedom at the convention for the National Council of Arts, Sciences, and Professions. But he soon became disillusioned with Progressivism's alliances with communism and announced at the Waldorf Peace Conference in New York that the Russian and American governments were equally imperialistic, equally bent on securing new markets for themselves by dominating backward countries. In 1962, to demonstrate against the desperate logic of nuclear bomb shelters, he stood in City Hall Park in New York and refused to take shelter during a civil defense drill. In 1967, participating in the antiwar march in Washington, he crossed the U.S. Marshalls' line and solitarily headed for the Pentagon. He was seized and arrested. In 1969 he announced his candidacy for mayor of New York. Running on a secessionist platform, he advocated that New York be made into the fifty-first state and that its neighborhoods effect self-governance. He came in a distant fourth in a field of five. In 1974 he founded the Fifth Estate, a citizen's organization established to investigate the activities of the CIA and the FBI.

We may cast these actions of Mailer under one ideological category or another, but, essentially, they go beyond politics. They have to do with something more important than politics—with, in fact, the individual's ambition to do battle with whatever fate society has designed for him and thereby to seize for himself a larger life.

The pattern of Norman Mailer's early life does not prefigure with any certainty the defiant eccentricities that come later. The first child and only son (he has a sister, Barbara) of Isaac Barnett Mailer and Fanny Schneider Mailer, he was born on January 31, 1923, in Long Branch, a resort town on New Jersey's north shore, where his mother's family was in the hotel business. Isaac Mailer, of Russian-Jewish extraction, served in the British army as a supply officer and emigrated to America from South Africa via London shortly after World War I. When his son was four years old, he moved his family to the Eastern Parkway section of Brooklyn, "the most secure Jewish environment in America," Mailer recalls.[3] Isaac (Barney) worked as an accountant in Brooklyn until his death in 1972. Mrs. Mailer still lives in Brooklyn and until recently ran a nursing and housekeeping service there. Barbara has worked from time to time as her brother's secretary. For a good part of Norman's writing career Barney and Fanny were practically his neighbors, living in a modest but comfortable apartment on Willow Street a block away from his Brooklyn Heights house, the main room of which—his study—is designed like a ship's forecastle and commands a magnificent view of the East River and the Lower Manhattan skyline.

Norman and Barbara received from their parents love, care, and the encouragement to succeed. That they both graduated with honors—Norman from Harvard and Barbara from Radcliffe—is one measure of their response to that encouragement. Norman "always had the highest marks," his mother recalls.[4] He was a confident youngster who played the clarinet and saxophone and spent untold hours building model airplanes. Aeronautics was his first love, but how interesting that as early as the age of nine he expressed this love in a literary way. He filled 250 notebook pages with a fantastical story called *An Invasion from Mars*. At Boys' High School in Brooklyn, Norman published his first work, an article on how to build model airplanes. Upon graduation he set his lights on M.I.T. and the study of aeronautical engineering. But because he was only sixteen, M.I.T. wanted him to go to prep school for an additional year. So he chose Harvard.

Once into his freshman year, he underwent probably the most profound change of his life. He discovered the modern American novel, immersing himself in his first semester in two trilogies, *Studs Lonigan* and *U.S.A.*, and *The Grapes of Wrath*. These were not just books read; they were experiences that happened to Mailer. They reshaped his mind and heart. He consecrated himself to writing, read Wolfe, Hemingway, and Faulkner, and vowed that he would become a major American novelist. A year later he wrote an unpublished novel, "No Percentage," about Jewish life in Brooklyn.

Mailer published his first short story, "The Greatest Thing in the World," in *The Harvard Advocate*. Derivative in conception, it is clearly written under the influence of his first masters: Farrell, Dos Passos, and Steinbeck. Encouraged by his writing professor, Robert Gorham Davis, he submitted the story to *Story* magazine's annual college contest and won first prize. Heady stuff for a sophomore. "The far away, all-powerful and fabulous world of New York publishing had said 'yes' to me."[5] Like all literary prizes, however, this one brought its weight of worry. Eighteen-year-old Truman Capote was already creating stories of consummate artistic beauty while Mailer feared that he was merely writing prose that "reads like the early work of a young man who is going to make a fortune writing first rate action, western, gangster, and suspense pictures."[6]

Life is not a movie, nor is it—for a young writer eager to recast the world in the crucible of his imagination—what other men, however great their talent, envision it to be. With these certitudes in mind, Mailer set out to garner some experiences on his own and allay his natural feelings of callowness. He took a job as an attendant at a state mental asylum in Boston during the summer before his senior year and wrote a play. After graduating from Harvard in 1943, he transformed the play into a novel. "A Transit to Narcissus" is a raw work seething with the brutalities and miseries that he observed at the asylum. It is

a romantic, morbid, twisted, and heavily tortured work which went possibly to twenty publishers before I realized that it was not going to be published. I mention it in this small detail because I suspect that if it had not been for the experience of the army (that invaluable experience for the writer of a situation which he cannot quit when he so chooses), I should have continued to write books in very much that style.[7]

The United States was twenty-eight months into its war with Japan when Mailer was inducted into the army in March 1944. That same month he married Beatrice Silverman of Chelsea, Massachusetts, who became a lieutenant in the WAVES (Women's Appointed Volunteer Emergency Service). Sent to the Pacific, Private Mailer became, by his own admission, "the third lousiest GI in a platoon of twelve."[8] Actually, he wasn't much interested in becoming a good soldier or a good patriot. Rather, he was obsessed with satisfying what he called that "cold maniacal thing in my heart, sharp as a shiv"—the desire to write the definitive American novel of World War II.[9] He went ashore with the U.S. infantry forces in the invasion of Luzon. Then, with his appointment to a desk job as a clerk-typist, the excitement came to a sudden stop. Eager to get the experience necessary to write his novel, he volunteered as a rifleman with a reconnaissance platoon fighting in the Philippine mountains. Nearly certain that he would not come out alive, he made sure that his novel would and wrote Bea four to five letters a week packed with voluminous notes.

After his discharge in April 1946, he and Beatrice rented a furnished, two-room apartment in Brooklyn (they had saved two thousand dollars) and settled down to writing. She too was writing a novel, but it was never published. Over the next fifteen months Mailer wrote with unflagging energy, averaging about thirty pages a week. He kept a large file of notes and a long dossier on each character. When the massive novel was finished, he and Bea left for Europe to study at the Sorbonne under the GI Bill of Rights. One day when Norman, Bea, and Barbara were returning from a motor trip in Italy, they stopped at the American Express office in Nice to check their mail. They were overwhelmed. Letters from friends and family beamed forth the news that *The Naked and the Dead* had become a spectacular success. The critical community had not seen such an auspicious debut for a novelist since the publication of Thomas Wolfe's *Look Homeward, Angel* in 1929. The novel headed the *New York Times* best-seller list for eleven consecutive weeks and sold 197,185 copies during its first year. Still a lad and still a student, Norman Mailer found himself the most celebrated young writer in America.

If we imagine literary apprenticeship as a time of bitter trial and error, then Mailer had none. But as much as he reveled in his success, it brought its share of woe. Indeed, one might say that his apprenticeship *began* with *The Naked and the Dead.* Not one to bare his soul in 1948, he told an interviewer, "These are rough times for little Normie," and let it go at that.[10] A decade later in *Advertisements for Myself* he was more specific: "Success had been a lobotomy to my past, there seemed no power from the past which could help me in the present, and I had no choice but to force myself to step into the war of the enormous present, to accept the private heat and fatigue of setting out by myself to cut a tract through a new wild."[11]

Cut loose from his old identity of nice-Jewish-boy-from-Brooklyn—an identity he had grown to hate—Mailer was now free to seek a new one. Always sympathetic to socialism, he entered first the realm of politics. But his espousal of Henry Wallace's bid for the presidency served only to bring him to the recognition that the end result of all governmental systems is oligarchic dominance. He traveled next to the realm of fantasy—to Hollywood, where he wrote an original screenplay for Metro-Goldwyn-Mayer. Sam Goldwyn rejected it, though he did offer to buy the script. Refusing Goldwyn's offer, Mailer tried to produce his screenplay independently, hoping to get Montgomery Clift and Charles Boyer to play the lead roles. But the venture failed. Concluding that fiction was his proper medium after all, he left the swampy marketplace of the movies and returned to the Parnassus of literature—to the East, where he wrote the greater part of his second novel (he had started it in Paris).

Deeply influenced by Jean Malaquais—the left-wing French intellectual who became Mailer's friend and guided him through the tortuous roadways of Marx's philosophy—*Barbary Shore* is an odd, febrile story of five desiccated lives caught between American and Soviet authoritarianism. Mailer wrote the book at an anguishing pitch, mining down into the darkest reaches of his self to come up with some starkly illuminating insights into the psyche of the fascist, the Trotskyite, the secret agent, the psychotic, the existentialist, and mass man. But the critics were not impressed. Those intent on upholding the puritanism of Eisenhower America called the book sordid. Others called it airless and ponderous. A divorce from Beatrice Silverman followed in its wake. A daughter, Susan, had been born in 1949.

For some time Mailer had been wanting to free himself from marriage and move into Greenwich Village, where, he imagined, a life of vibrant bohemianism awaited him. He felt that after several years of hard work and continence, he owed himself the adventurous pleasures that ought to accrue to a famous young man. When a friend introduced him to the beautiful Adele Morales, a Spanish-Peruvian painter, he found at last the world of lavish excitement he had been missing. Adele brightened his life and loosened him up. They were married in 1954. In the same year Mailer founded, with Daniel Wolf and Edwin Fancher, *The Village Voice*, a pioneering weekly newspaper on politics and the arts.

But Mailer's Greenwich Village period soon changed from gladness to turbulence. He began to fuel his brain with stimulants of higher and higher potency—liquor, marijuana, benzedrine, seconal—and to court, sometimes with Adele, orgiastic ecstasies. Such experimentation took its physical toll—appendicitis and a damaged liver. It seemed as though Mailer would almost rather have died than continue to live within the bounds of normative reality, for he was convinced that his journeyings into the dens of forbidden desire had put him in possession of something akin to Dionysian knowledge. According to Daniel Wolf, Mailer had "stopped being concerned about

being a writer, and become much more concerned as
a bringer of truth."[12] He had now become a polemicist
expounding the subversive philosophy of Hip—his
own special amalgam of the thought of Reich, Sartre,
and Marx. What Mailer "wanted at the time," says
Wolf, "was a big explosion that would make the scene.
He felt that if you just pressed the right button, all
these people would come up from The Underground"
and he would lead them in a revolution aimed at the
annihilation of every smug tradition of American life
—security, monogamy, organization, patriotism, capitalism.[13] But the people did not come up.

In the midst of his delusion, his recklessness, and
what he thought of as his sloth, Mailer set out to write
a novel that he hoped would regain for him the
distinction he lost with the publication of *Barbary
Shore*. Lashed by ambition, he committed himself over
a four-year period to the exhaustive writing and
rewriting of *The Deer Park*, a novel about the symbolic
hell of a Hollywood resort and the venal people in
it. The book's publication met with mixed reviews.
It was only a partial success, which, on Mailer's
competitive scale of all or nothing, meant a failure.
His reaction was dire. He became a literary outlaw.
Because the world had not, he believed, tried to
understand him, he resolved that he would no longer
try to understand the world. Rather, he would turn
inward to explore, as incisively as he knew how, the
tremors and desires of his own psyche in such a way
that one would come to believe it was America's
psyche itself, if not one's own character, that was being
explored. He succeeded. *Advertisements for Myself*,
a virtuosic striptease of the mind, established Mailer
as a writer of searing candor and oracular brilliance.
He became *philosophe maudit* to the nation.

Yet the turmoil of his personal life continued. In
1960, after a demonic all-night party at their new

Manhattan apartment, he stabbed his wife Adele with
a penknife, seriously wounding her, and entered
Bellevue hospital for seventeen days of psychiatric
observation. His wife did not press charges; she re-
covered and they were soon reconciled. But in 1962
he and Adele were divorced. They had two daughters,
Danielle and Elizabeth Anne. That same year he
married Lady Jeanne Campbell, daughter of the Duke
of Argyll and granddaughter of Lord Beaverbrook, the
Canadian-born financier and newspaper magnate. His
marriage with Lady Jeanne was calamitous and short.
After a year, in which a daughter, Kate, was born,
they were divorced, and Mailer promptly married the
actress Beverly Bentley. What an astonishing departure
all this is from the soft-voiced young man who said
in 1948, "Actually, I've got all the average middle-class
fears."[14] Now Mailer had become the terrible ruffian
of American letters.

For sensation-seeking journalists he became little
more than material for racy copy. Arrested in Provincetown for calling "Taxi!" several times to a police
cruiser, he tussles with the arresting officers, suffers a
considerable cut on the head, is thrown in jail—then
undertakes his own defense in court and gets himself
acquitted; in a televised interview with Mike Wallace,
he suggests that juvenile delinquency in New York
can be decreased by holding once a year a medieval
jousting tournament in Central Park between members
of rival gangs; he is arrested at Birdland, a New York
nightclub, for bellicosely trying to pay for his liquor
bill with credit; reciting his lascivious, grimly lyrical
poetry at the Lexington Avenue Y.M.H.A. Poetry
Series, he has the curtain brought down on him for
alleged obscenity; in Chicago, after Sonny Liston
knocks out Floyd Patterson, he confronts the bearish
Liston and tells him to wise up and let him promote
his next fight; he finances José Torres's championship

bid for the world light-heavyweight championship and later dons a pair of boxing gloves himself to go four rounds with Torres on the Dick Cavett television show. If the above acts are exhibitionistic or absurd, Mailer does not object because they are his ways of being a writer, and, by his logic, if they help him to write well, they cannot be so very foolish. Much madness is divinest sense.

Just how objectionable Mailer's behavior is depends then, in large part, on one's estimation of his writing, which, interestingly, has become more compelling since his emergence as a public personality. With *The Presidential Papers* and *Cannibals and Christians*, he developed a reputation as an astute critic of politics and society in America. With *The Armies of the Night* (winner of the National Book Award and the Pulitzer Prize) and *Miami and the Siege of Chicago*, he gained an international reputation for a dramatic rendering of the same subjects. His two novels, *An American Dream* and *Why Are We in Vietnam?*, project the daydreams and subliminal compulsions of the American character with tonal colorations never before seen in American fiction.

Living and reporting the historic stresses of the 1960s, Mailer began to suspect that our national reality had become more fantastical than any fiction could imagine it. His suspicion was confirmed by NASA's announcement that it was ready to rocket man to the moon. Commissioned by *Life* magazine, he flew to Houston and Cape Kennedy to cover the flight of Apollo 11. As spectacular, though, as Mailer believes the moon shot is in *Of a Fire on the Moon*, he holds that the cosmic forces of existence just as provocatively, just as sublimely, emerge within the relationship between man and woman as within the infinite reaches of space. Mailer contends that the interplay between the sexes is a process that God has ordained to bring symmetry and balance to Creation. The heterosexual relationship "is one of the prime symbols of the connection between all things."[15]

In recent years the chief experiences in Mailer's life have concerned women. In 1970 he separated from his fourth wife, Beverly Bentley, and their two sons— Michael Burks and Stephen McLeod. That same year leading exponents of the new feminists denounced him as the principal voice of male chauvinism on the American literary scene. He counterattacked with a comically trenchant treatise, *The Prisoner of Sex.* Yet *Marilyn*, a biography of Marilyn Monroe, is a memorial to Woman. The exaltations, the agonies, the dreams inherent in a man's and a woman's knowledge of each other have formed much of the substance of Mailer's life and work. Jazz singer Carol Stevens, Mailer's companion after his separation from Beverly Bentley, bore him a daughter, Maggie, in 1971. Five years later he and Ms. Stevens separated.

Today Mailer divides his time between a cottage in Provincetown, Massachusetts, and his brownstone house in Brooklyn Heights. He tries to keep his days free from interference. He must, for in 1974 he signed a one million dollar contract with Little, Brown to write a novel of at least two and possibly five volumes. To date he has written 200,000 words. A work of mythic themes, a family saga ranging back into ancient times and forward into the future, it will take five to seven years to complete. Part of the book is set in ancient Egypt, about the 20th Dynasty, and part takes place in a spaceship. Some of it concerns the life of a Jewish family before World War I. A good deal of it will be contemporary. Reluctant to talk about the novel, Mailer has admitted to this much: ". . . I like to stick with something that has a lot to do with the structure of, oh, I don't know, the way time works. It's really going to be, to a certain extent, a full

cyclical work, if that isn't too pompous."[16] Recently
he divulged a little, but not much, more: "I'm trying
to create periods of time which look at one another
like characters, or maybe it's better to say like forces
which attract and repel each other. But I've already
said too much."[17] Those who have read the novel in
manuscript have described it as Jungian, Tolstoyan.
And it seems likely that the religious philosophy of
karma, which has deeply interested Mailer in recent
years, will be an underlying theme.

One million dollars is not as abundant a figure
as it seems because, as Mailer readily admits, four
ex-wives and seven children constitute a family enter-
prise of costly proportions. Nor do his expenses stop
there; his accountant, his agent, his lawyer, and his
government must be paid. He speaks from woeful
experience when he says, "Economics is half of literature."[18] Little, Brown has given him the chance now to
keep in the black the better to apply himself to that
one grand objective that he has been trying to attain
for the past twenty years:

. . . to hit the longest ball ever to go up into the accelerated
hurricane air of our American letters. For if I have one
ambition above all others, it is to write a novel which
Dostoyevsky and Marx; Joyce and Freud; Stendhal,
Tolstoy, Proust, and Spengler; Faulkner, and even old
moldering Hemingway might come to read, for it would
carry what they had to tell another part of the way.[19]

Judging by Mailer's work thus far, and by what he is
as a man, we may not be mistaken in expecting that
this new novel will be a fusion—in what ways we
cannot yet know—of vitality, frankness, dread, egotism, metaphysics, sensuality, occultism, pretension,
passion, and cunning. Forged into unified form, these
qualities cannot but produce the most disruptively
prodigious novel that we have seen in a very long
while.

2

○○

Thwarted Will:
The Naked and the Dead

In 1944 twenty-one-year-old Norman Mailer joined the army with one thought uppermost in his mind—to write *the* American novel of World War II. Sent to the Philippines as an artillery surveyor, he served in the campaigns at Leyte and Luzon. Assigned to intelligence at combat headquarters, he typed battle reports and interpreted aerial photographs, gaining thereby a general's view of the war. Intent on seeing the face of battle, he transferred to the 112th Cavalry, a Texas National Guard outfit, and fought as a rifleman behind enemy lines outside Manila. He served his last overseas assignment as a cook with the occupation forces in Japan. In 1946 he returned to the United States and wrote *The Naked and the Dead*. Never before had an American writer so single-mindedly set about the task of amassing a body of experience and shaping from his imaginative grasp of that experience material with which to write a novel. Mailer finished the book in fifteen months. It rushed out of him in a storm of creativity and achieved a remarkable critical and popular success. A modest ex-infantryman became the most talked-about new writer in America. He was twenty-five.

The Naked and the Dead tells the story of a fourteen-man infantry platoon that lands on the barren beach of Anopopei, a small Japanese-held island in the South Pacific. The platoon is part of a six-thousand-man force charged with the task of seizing control of the island in order to clear the way for a larger American advance into the Philippines. Tightly unified, this 721-page novel adheres to the classic plot structure of introduction, rising action, climax, falling action, and denouement.

The opening pages reveal the enlisted men as they crouch in the troop-ship hold tremulously waiting to charge upon the beach. Mailer carefully delineates their differences—emotional, geographic, social, economic—because he intends them to constitute a microcosmic portrait of the American populace. The *dramatis personae* include a God-fearing Mississippi dirt farmer; a sensitive Jew from Brooklyn; a socially oppressed Mexican-American; a sullen, demonic west Texas rancher; an embittered itinerant laborer from the coal mines of Montana; a reactionary Irishman from South Boston's working class; a dull, middle-class Kansas salesman; a cynical Chicago hoodlum; a dissipated hedonist from Georgia.

The rising action concerns the execution of General Edward Cummings's key battle strategy against the Toyaku Line (named after the Japanese commander). He assigns his staff officer, Lieutenant Robert Hearn, the task of leading the platoon through the south jungle of Anopopei on a reconnaissance mission behind the Toyaku Line. Midway in the patrol's incursion, an enemy sniper shoots Private Wilson in the belly and four men attempt to carry him back to safety on a makeshift litter. Two of the bearers eventually give up in exhaustion, but Ridges and Goldstein—the religiously devout sharecropper and the ridiculed, ungainly Jew—complete the trek over muddy hills, across baked fields of kunai grass, and through suffocating jungle, where Wilson finally dies.

Minutes later Ridges and Goldstein lose his body in the swirling rapids of a river.

Meanwhile, the patrol slowly and perilously advances. Enemy machine-gun fire kills Lieutenant Hearn, and Corporal Roth hurtles to his death trying to leap across a ledge. The patrol, now only half its original size and under the ruthless leadership of Sergeant Sam Croft, struggles doggedly toward the peak of Mount Anaka, the majestic mountain that rises from the island's center and protects the rear of the Toyaku Line. When the patrol nearly attains the summit, a nest of hornets—nature's blind nemesis— explodes upon it. Like flaming hail, the hornets sweep down upon the men. They stumble, run, and fall down the mountain slope.

Unaware that the patrol has failed, General Cummings briefly leaves the island to consult with high command. He appoints the obtuse, bureaucratic Major Dalleson "in charge of operations" during his absence. Dalleson intends to sit tight and keep all troops stationary until the general's return, but when a scouting squad reports to him that a breach has been discovered in the Toyaku Line, he has no choice but to order a battalion through it. The battalion stumbles straight into a major Japanese supply depot and destroys it. A few hundred yards beyond, it discovers and destroys the Japanese secret headquarters that houses General Toyaku and his staff. The novel's climax, then, is a victory for the U.S. Army, but a personal defeat for Cummings. His masterful battle plan has counted for naught. A fateful fluke has at once dictated men's lives—made heroes of a few, cynics and malcontents of many, corpses of the rest— and rendered intelligent forethought useless.

The novel's denouement consists of "mopping up" activities. The American forces wipe out the last weak pockets of Japanese resistance, and it appears later that the Japanese army had been teetering on the brink of collapse for weeks. The men of the patrol rejoin their regiment and seemingly dissolve within it; they become anonymous. Their harrowing struggle has been, as Mailer metaphorically imagines it, an evanescent swell in the ocean of time. That swell has been scrupulously limned from its initial "Wave" (Part One) to its final "Wake" (Part Four).

Over the perspective of both officers and enlisted men prevails the narrative voice of Mailer, who, Olympian-like, remains a detached, omniscient observer. He conveys the tribulations of war with almost scathing objectivity. Though his prose recalls the clarity and precision of Steinbeck's *Grapes of Wrath*, the stance he takes toward his characters resembles that of Dos Passos in his *U.S.A.* trilogy. Mailer refuses to allow us to get involved with a character or to imagine that any man has control over the historical moment in which he finds himself. Once we draw sympathetically close to someone, the narrative shifts to another character or scene. In the case of Hearn, for example, we draw near only to be cut off from him with a sudden notice of his death: "A half-hour later, Hearn was killed by a machine-gun bullet which passed through his chest." It seems that only the grimmest of interpretations can be made. In a dumb, wanton universe man labors to die. He does not really fit into the universe; he is an outlaw on an earth not designed for him. In a profoundly anti-Christian vein, we conclude that God does not take any interest in man.

The title of Part Two, "Argil and Mold," distills Mailer's world view. Argil is white potter's clay—the human being before he is molded by the familial, social, and economic forces that inexorably determine his personality. To give dramatic form to this meta-

phor, Mailer dispenses throughout his narrative ten
"Time Machine" sequences, or flashbacks, in which
he records the personal history of his main characters
and thereby shows us how they have come to be what
they are. A montage of poetic prose and reportorial
realism, each Time Machine dramatizes the pathetic
endeavors of human hope "arrayed against the casual,
ugly attrition of time." Mailer envisions time as a
cosmic engine—an infinite, mechanized matrix of
cause and effect which enmeshes man. Together, the
Time Machines form a panorama of a contaminated
America, one in which social privilege, exploitation,
poverty, racial bigotry, and sexual decadence burgeon
forth in terrible abundance.

Clearly, Mailer's perspective in this novel seems
noninnovational for it is derived from naturalism, the
prevailing point of view of the American masters of
the 1930s—Steinbeck, Dos Passos, Farrell, and
Hemingway—who inspired him. Naturalism's most
frequent metaphor, the lawless jungle, is the literal
setting of *The Naked and the Dead.* In the naturalistic
world, the individual is prey to certain forces over
which he has no full knowledge or control. These
forces are biological (Wilson's sexual drives), social
(Martinez's ardent striving to be included in WASP
society), and geographical (the almost impervious
jungle and the taunting grandeur of Mount Anaka).

It remains, however, that the compelling dramatic
tension of this novel—the very wellspring of its dark
vitality—derives from Mailer's fascination with the
lives of three men—Cummings, Croft, and Hearn—
who daringly try to press their wills upon necessity.
In their efforts to define themselves in opposition to a
deterministic universe, we find all that Mailer held
to be of moral value at this stage in his career. Their
significance has much to do with what he wrote in
his final column for *The Village Voice* in 1956: "Man's

nature, man's dignity, is that he acts, lives, loves, and
finally destroys himself seeking to penetrate the
mystery of existence, and unless we partake in some
way, as some part of this human exploration (and war)
then we are no more than the pimps of society and the
betrayers of our Self." Cummings, Croft, and Hearn
have the dignity of those who seek to penetrate the
mystery of existence. Despite their differences, the
same unarticulated ethic guides them all: what one
gets out of life depends upon what *one gets*, not upon
what is given—be it the love of a woman or societal
favor or whatever. They are committed to defining
themselves by their own inner lights, not in accordance
with any exterior measure. Their lives, in short, are
existential.

Mailer's characterization of Cummings is ambivalent. The general has a brilliant mind, yet uses it
primarily for self-aggrandizement; his self-discipline,
while unflagging, cannot be distinguished from his
Napoleonic pride. The command of six thousand men
stirs him with demagogic ecstasy. He is obsessed with
consolidating for himself all the power he can so that
he may become a leader in the fascist world of the
future. The "only morality of the future," he tells
Hearn, "is a power morality, and a man who cannot
find his adjustment to it is doomed." He predicts that
after the war America will establish a foreign policy
of outright, unhypocritical imperialism.

His aberrant egotism repulses Mailer—but greatly
interests him. For in Cummings he sees a part of
himself. The general sitting alone at night in his tent
mapping out his attack strategy while the bivouacked
men outside idly chatter and complain symbolizes
Mailer's conception of himself as the cloistered artist.
He identifies his own struggle to forge a novel from
a collection of uncorrelated ideas and imaginings with
Cummings's brooding efforts to design a battle plan

from the diverse elements of a tired, obstinate army. Cummings's mind—like the artist's—is demiurgic; for it recombines and reshapes the phenomena of raw reality to engender a meaningful, living, new reality. The creative will makes from lumpen formlessness vital form. General Cummings represents, then, Mailer's self-projection of himself as the Romantic artist convinced that he is possessed of the ability to recreate the world.

Sergeant Sam Croft—the general's emotional twin —is also obsessed with finding a channel for unrealized power. They are dynamic, refractory men who comprehend evil as ineradicable yet somehow vital. Their very awareness of such evil gives them an energy the other men do not possess. Croft's traits—his cruelty and courage, his contempt for others, and his extraordinary stamina—interfuse. They are of a piece. Through his characterization of Croft, Mailer advances his monistic theory of personality, which proposes that all dualistic views are myopic. Once we free ourselves from dissecting, moralistic perceptions, there is only undifferentiated being. Mailer intends us to believe that if Croft's devils were to leave him, his angels would surely follow. For all of Croft's wanton violence —he seizes a bird from Corporal Roth's sheltering hands and squeezes it to death; he cold-bloodedly kills a Japanese prisoner—he is the ablest soldier in the book. He is more self-reliant, more tenacious, more resilient—more *alive*—than any other character.

Mailer never forgot certain squad leaders he met while serving in the Philippines. From his comments on them in *Advertisements for Myself* we can understand Croft in a clearer light:

None of us had the slightest desire to be killed in an action which could not even give a good marble of fact to the ponderous idiots who directed our fate, the squad leader was no more anxious than we were to get knocked off that

way, but if he had a bit of the artist in him, and the good
ones always did, he would gamble on his perception
because it was the only way for him to grow. If he did
not take the high hill he would never find out if his
suspicion that Japanese might be there was good or wrong,
and so whenever he would next have to call on a collobora-
tion between his paranoia and his courage, his instincts
would be slack with untested questions. A good squad
leader looked for a bit of trouble to keep himself cool, and
it was remarkable how seldom one ran into ambush.

What sets Croft apart from the other men—
Cummings and Hearn included—is that where he is
characterized by *rebellion*, they are characterized by
resentment.[1] For Mailer there is a qualitative difference between the two. Every man but Croft seethes
with resentment, festers in a condition of prolonged
impotence. And always this resentment turns into
either unscrupulous ambition (Corporal Stanley's hyp-
ocritical toadying, Private Czienwicz's racketeering)
or bitterness (Red Valsen's angry resignation before
the forces of authority, Corporal Roth's indignant
snobbery). Resentment in this novel is like a sealed
vessel fermenting with envy, while rebellion breaks
the seal and allows the whole being to come into play.
Each of the men wants to be something other than
what he is. While the rebel's aim—Croft's aim—is to
defend what he is, to possess something he has and
which has already been recognized by him as more
important than anything of which he could be envious.
Resentment, as Mailer dramatizes it, is always resentment against oneself. But the rebel, on the contrary,
from the very start, refuses to allow anyone to touch
him. He fights for the integrity of his being. He does
not try primarily to conquer, but simply to impose, to
affirm his own solidarity in the onrush of happenstance.

The image of Mount Anaka brings these motivations of Croft into stark focus. The whole action of the

novel is somehow foreshadowed and gathered around
this absorbing reference point. When Croft sees the
mountain in all its cold sublimity—its peak lofting
massively into a translucent crown of clouds—and
undertakes to lead the reconnaissance patrol over its
heights, his rebellion attains archetypal proportions.
For in climbing Mount Anaka, Croft intends to confirm
that he is not what the mountain, in its aloof splendor,
seems to say he is: mere flesh, a weak, transitory
creature. The mountain symbolizes to Croft that whole
array of deific qualities—immortality, spiritual transcendence, immutable fate, eternity—which mock
man's mortality and which the noblest of men try
valiantly to understand or attain. To scale Mount
Anaka means to him—and, by extension, to all mankind—that human flesh is more than mere flesh, that
it possesses the same mystical strengths the mountain
does.

When Croft fails to reach the summit, he despairs
in the knowledge that his hunger was delusive. We
must conclude that the mountain's spirituality is
wholly impersonal. Man may be *in* nature—for Mailer
he is entrapped in it, embroiled in it—but he is not *of*
it. No intimate kinship exists between man and nature.
Man has no soul, only nature does. Like Hemingway's
Kilimanjaro, Mount Anaka's austere grandeur per-
petually reminds man of his woefully confining
mortality. Like Melville's White Whale, it is mysterious, fearful, and beckoning. Its meaning calls to mind
the words of the British scientist J.S.B. Haldane. "My
own suspicion is that the universe is not only queerer
than we suppose, but queerer than we can suppose."[2]
Haldane's "suspicion" may have excited him, and it
certainly does Mailer in his later career. In the world
of his early fiction, however, it can cause only distress,
for it leaves man feeling helpless and absurd.

As the distant peak of Mount Anaka remains

unattainable, so does man's knowledge of himself.
And Judaic-Christian values can be of no help. Goldstein and Ridges—because of an abiding faith instilled
by religious ethic—persevere to the end in carrying
the wounded Wilson. But regeneration or self-
discovery does not attend their struggle. What makes
this novel so disturbing is not the actual horror of war,
but Mailer's unrelenting vision of the void—of the
lack of love, justice, and mercy. Nothing human is
sacred, and the only constant is change. The unpre-
dictable oscillations of nature and man's emotions
charge every scene. To be human is to be a mass of
uncorrelated impulses. Life is irrevocably problem-
atical, whether intensely examined (Cummings) or
intensely experienced (Croft).

The connecting link between the fascistic Cummings and the demonic Croft is Lieutenant Robert
Hearn, a liberal and a skeptic and the only character
who attains a genuine understanding of what Mailer's
title means. The phrase "the naked and the dead"
constitutes the novel's basic thematic statement.
"Naked" means that man is unaccommodated, without
covering in the face of fate; he is without dependable
support in a universe that reveals to him only one
certainty—his destiny, which is death. Hearn's perceptions mirror Mailer's. Not surprisingly, items in Hearn's
background parallel items in Mailer's: Harvard, a
fling at house football, intellectual cynicism, a serious
affair with leftist politics, a hungry interest in the
literary masters, and short-story writing.

Contrary to most men, Hearn does not seek power,
money, or social prominence, and, unlike Cummings
and Croft, he is unable to sublimate his wayward
impulses into purposeful action. Yet, despite his in-
effectiveness, he never capitulates to the stock-in-trade
ideologies of the powers that be—neither to the
capitalistic elitism of the class from which he originates

nor to the autocratic position of General Cummings. He sees through every certitude, forswears allegiance to all camps, and resists their courting. Officers Conn and Dove, for example, would invite Hearn to share in the privileged comforts of their class and rank if he were not so repulsed by their smug parochialism. He would rather be alienated than have to choose a belief that does not spring from his own personal needs. His prewar milieu recalls the social arena of F. Scott Fitzgerald's fiction. Amid the partying and falseness of New York's upper classes, Hearn, like the Fitzgeraldian hero (both of whom are scions of the Midwest), lives at a level others cannot understand, possessed, as he is, of a painfully unfulfilled sense of duty and conduct.

Cummings is an example of what Dostoyevsky called "titanism." A static belief in unqualified power motivates his introspection. For Hearn, however, the primary value of introspection—its very grace—is that it can liberate the individual not only from the tyranny of his culture but from the tyranny of his own need for power, and permit him to stand beyond both in the flexibility of intellect and imagination. Hearn, of course, never fully realizes this ideal, but he does move toward it, even despite his passing desire "to become like Croft."

Cummings, Croft, and Hearn, without losing their individuality, approximate modern incarnations of three great heroes of western civilization. Cummings, in his overweening urge to shape reality to his own needs and make the world answerable to them, represents Faustian man. Croft, in his irrepressible desire to attain to the vast strength of Mount Anaka, resembles the Satanic hero. And Hearn, in his dispassionate rejection of everything that would impose conditions on the autonomy of his thought, approaches Socratic man. The mythic heroism of these three men and the naturalistic universe they oppose is the primary dramatic conflict in *The Naked and the Dead*. In artistic terms, the conflict is between romance and realism. The interplay between these two elements gives this novel its identifying form as a work of art.

The other men who fill out Mailer's portrait of the human story possess varying degrees of virtue but essentially are made of common clay. They can neither accept things as they literally are nor escape them through action. Gallagher cannot see beyond the stifling provincialism of the lower-class Boston Irishry from which he springs. Wilson's uncontrollable sexual appetite results in syphilis. Brown is an insipid product of the beliefs of America's middle class. Red cannot successfully rebel against authority, symbolized by Croft. Martinez will always remain outside the "firm and aloof" WASP precincts he dreams of entering. Czienwicz believes that personal fulfillment will attend his next theft or con job. The Jews Goldstein and Roth congratulate themselves on their sympathies and intellect, yet both are unable to fruitfully manifest these qualities in their relations with others. They founder in isolating sensitivity.

Self-absorption, however, does not typify Goldstein and Roth alone. It is the indelible attribute of every man in the platoon. Even women cannot wrest them from isolation, mainly because these men do not know what to do with women except take them to bed. Though effective in assuaging loneliness, inferiority, and anger, women are, finally, only bromides for these conditions. Mailer characterizes the male-female relationship as delusory; it is temporarily fulfilling and then permanently disillusioning; marital boredom follows amorous release. The pattern of love is self-defeating; when man gets the woman he longs for, he soon develops a gnawing sense of self-waste.

Mailer's vision of the heterosexual relationship

may be read as the paradigm of a yet more ultimate law: any travail amounts to naught. Cummings's masterful battle plan exemplifies this law. Victory occurs despite, not because of, the general's strategy. The novel ends with Major Dalleson's success and his cry of *"Hot dog!"* His gross lack of imagination has in no way impeded his victory. In fact, his very dullness has enabled him to plod through to success in a situation in which a percipient man would pause to consider overviews and consequences until it was too late effectively to act. Mailer's pessimism runs deep: it says that banality prevails in American life not because men of original intelligence do not exist—the novel clearly shows that they do—but because there is no tenable place for them in society. Dalleson's rallying cry is the hot dog, that ubiquitous symbol of American mediocrity and meretriciousness.

The reader, however, might be more willing to accept the terms of Mailer's vision were it not for a certain heavy-handedness in his tone. Plainly God, equality, purity, and charity do not exist in the novel, but occasionally Mailer overemphasizes the point. Here, for example, is a description from a Time Machine of Roy Gallagher and his wife Mary on the Beach at City Point, Boston:

> City Point is so beautiful, she says.
> In the night they cannot see the garbage that litters the beach, seaweed and driftwood, the condoms that wallow sluggishly at the foam's edge, discarded on the shore like the minuscule loathsome animals of the sea.

The emphasis on the condoms seems gratuitous. In trying to avoid sentimentality, Mailer has gone too far to the other side and presented us with undue rawness.

The Time Machine sections do not always ring true. Mailer has portrayed his characters with full realistic detail, but the reader is likely to feel that his depictions are based on stereotypes. The settings compel our belief, but, except for Mailer's treatment of Joey Goldstein's Brooklyn, we sense that he has never lived in them.

Still, the novel's flaws fall reasonably within the framework of a highly distinguished achievement. *The Naked and the Dead* has been wrought out of an urgent pressure to give honest expression to experience. Mailer has forged a hard, plain, pungent prose. The verbs are strong, the nouns precise, the adjectives evocative; and almost never does a stylistic flourish or a facile observation obtrude between the reader and the subject:

Wilson's wound was throbbing painfully. The muscles in his stomach were sore and exhausted from fighting against the pain, and a dry fever had settled in his body. Under the sun all his limbs had become leaden and aching, his chest and throat congested, completely dry. Each jolt of the stretcher shocked him like a blow. He felt the exhaustion of having fought against a man much bigger than himself, much stronger than himself for many hours. He teetered often on the edge of unconsciousness, but always he would be jarred back into his pain by a sudden wrench of the litter. It brought him close to weeping.

Avoiding the slickness of *The Young Lions* and the sentimentality of *From Here to Eternity*, *The Naked and the Dead* is the finest novel in English to come out of World War II. More than any particular philosophy or social theory it may advance, its claim to greatness lies in the fact that Mailer defines war on the raw, sensate level and thereby makes us understand it in a palpable way. The novel's true impact derives from the felt immediacy of its images. War is a spasm in the stomach, the heart's twisted, knotted movements, the blood, thick and quick, washing within the skull, the severe discomfort of bivouacs, the misery of long marches, the frustration of not knowing where you are or where you are going. These things go beyond ideation. They make the novel an *experience*.

As a young novelist starting out, Mailer chose war as his subject convinced that only in a crisis situation could man's real nature be bared. The great value of his achievement is that in doing so he revealed two age-old human tensions—the struggle between animal desire and spiritual aspiration, the struggle between individualism and authority—in their essential pattern, and with a power, a gravity, and a veracity never before seen in the American novel. The plight of the reconnaissance patrol works a catharsis upon the reader. Three hundred pages of rattled nerves, quivering fatigue, fevered plodding, and searing disillusionment deplete us. We are roused and drained and driven to a rare pitch of truth. A hammering scrutiny of life's damage leaves us with an earnest respect for the people who must sustain it, and, on a deeper level, we release a sardonic sigh about the blunders of our own life, exempting ourselves from pity toward others, while renouncing it for ourselves.

3

○○○○○○○○○○○○○○○○○○○○○○○○○○○○○○○○○○○○

Apocalyptic Politics:
Barbary Shore

Mailer's second novel, *Barbary Shore*, is narrated by an amnesiac. Having suffered a head wound in World War II, Michael Lovett is now rootless and desensitized. Bereft of belief, often of even a point of view, he can remember nothing certain of his past except that he grew up in an orphanage and was "always poor."

The action of the novel takes place around 1950 in a dingy, run-down rooming house on the cliffs of Brooklyn Heights that overlook the East River. This is Mailer's barbary shore, to which Lovett has come to write a novel—"a large ambitious work about an immense institution never defined more exactly than that, and about the people who wander through it." The novel has a hero and heroine who never meet while they are in the institution. When they escape, each by separate methods, they meet and fall in love. Lovett's proposed novel is, whether consciously intended or not, analogous to George Orwell's futuristic *1984*, which was published in 1949 and very much in the literary air at the time Mailer was writing this book. Like stories by Dostoyevsky, Gide, and Huxley, *Barbary Shore* is a novel about the making of a novel.

It is not coincidental that Willie Dinsmore, himself a writer, sublets his room to Lovett. One suspects that Willie believes the rooming house will be to

Lovett what it quite probably was to him—a novelistic laboratory, a place that will provide him, in the lives of the people at close reach, raw material for a book. Lovett is a detached sideline observer. But as the novel progresses, he is increasingly drawn into the clash of events he records.

In the rooming house Lovett meets five people: Guinivere, the voluptuous landlady with whom he has a short affair; Monina, her strange, impish child; Lannie, a haunted, Cassandra-like girl who, once committed to Russia's revolution, underwent torturous shock-treatment during the days of the Stalinist purges; McLeod, a former Trotskyite and later a secret agent for Stalin; Hollingsworth, a dull-headed rightist spy from the Midwest sent by an unknown organization, possibly the FBI or the CIA, to investigate McLeod.

The dramatic core of the novel consists of Hollingsworth's efforts to maneuver McLeod into a confession of his communistic alignments. McLeod, it seems, once operated within the highest ranks of the party hierarchy, but since the Stalinist purges has divorced himself from the party and gone into hiding. Hollingsworth's investigation hinges on the successful search for the "little lost object," which McLeod allegedly has in his possession. It is never discovered, so one can only guess at its identity. On the symbolic level, however, it represents—for McLeod, and finally for Lovett—the egalitarian principles of the socialist cause; whoever possesses it is responsible for bearing the torch in the coming socialist revolution. In the end, the federal police invade the rooming house, and we last see Lovett running down a dark alley. It was McLeod's hope that Lovett would eventually carry the socialist doctrine to the world at large, but Lovett seems to know no more about how to do this than most of us do.

Somewhat like Dostoyevsky's narrator in *Notes*

from Underground, Lovett is an urban self-exile holed up in cheap lodgings and groping for meaning in restless anonymity. But the essential difference between the "underground man" and Lovett is that while Dostoyevsky's character, despite the meaninglessness of his life, was aggressively willful, Lovett is passive. In fact, he does not seem to be a living *presence* at all.

It would be simplistic to say that Lovett is not real for us because he is not real to himself. The problem, really, lies with the book's artistry. Mailer has set himself a difficult task—to make a pallid character engaging. *Barbary Shore* represents Mailer's first first-person narration, and he has not quite mastered the form. The prose is articulate, but flat. Lovett's vapidity is essentially a function of his characterization, not of his character.

There is intensity of mood only in the last third of the novel when Lovett loses interest in his affair with Guinivere and befriends McLeod. The atmosphere changes from nervous stagnation to conspiratorial tension, and McLeod becomes the focus of the story. His impassioned monologues on the contemporary world—its politics, its economics, its social structures—constitute Mailer's vision of reality at midcentury.

McLeod is the percipient eye of the novel. In a few phrases he can tell us more about Lovett than Lovett can tell us about himself: the narrator is a "crippled prig," a "blunted flattened spirit, . . . a castrate in short." In their last discussion together, McLeod accuses Lovett of being a "poor little monk" with "patches showing in your frock, and nothing left to yourself so that you can only sup for emotional wares at someone else's table." More starved for life than he knows, Lovett is even willing to commit himself to the mentally disturbed Lannie in a desperate try for some kind of emotional connection. But Mc-

Leod's appraisal of him is far from negative. He
recognizes that Lovett has a knowledge of socialist
dialectic, and while Lovett may not be as wise as
McLeod, the latter perceives in him the voice of
conscience. Lovett represents to McLeod decency, the
common man cutting his precarious way through a
world of deceit and corruption.

The governing tone of *Barbary Shore* is one of
desperation; the rooming house is "desperation alley."
Everyone in Mailer's bleak house seems to corroborate
McLeod's dark knowledge: the world is foredoomed
to holocaust because war is an economic necessity.
McLeod apocalyptically forecasts that "the intent of
society will be to produce wholly for death, and men
will be kept alive merely to further that aim." McLeod
and Lannie, stripped by Trotsky's failed counterrevolu-
tion of all hope for themselves and for humankind,
await the violent future in helpless bitterness.

Though the novel's setting is insular, even claus-
trophobic, its outlook is international. After the sexual
drama in the first half of the book between Lovett and
Guinivere and then between Lovett and Lannie,
Mailer, through the disquisitions of McLeod, turns
his book into a political commentary on the state of
the world.

Lovett melts into the background, and the novel
becomes McLeod's story. Structurally this causes a
disjointed effect. The plot and pace of the novel slow
down, and we are left with pure discourse.

McLeod's central proposition is that the United
States and the Soviet Union are both exploitative
oligarchies. Their industries are enforced labor camps
in disguise wherein the worker produces well beyond
the worth of his wage. As McLeod sees it, the United
States and the Soviet Union are brothers under the
skin, and the ideals of the Revolution of 1917 were
betrayed. Expanding production compels state capi-

talism, be it American or Russian, to control foreign markets. Given the economic requirements of state capitalism, war is imperative. As a consequence of war, one country vanquishes another. But both the victorious and the defeated country find themselves impoverished because of a decrease in armament manufacture and an increase in unemployment caused by a returning army. To survive they become imperialistic and exploit new countries, stripping them of their wealth. The novel's title takes its name from the ensuing situation: "The war begins again with a new alignment of forces, and to the accompaniment of famine and civil war, the deterioration continues until we are faced with mankind in barbary." Adding details to his central proposition, McLeod demolishes anything that can be said in support of American or Soviet government. He then offers his outline for a beneficent socialist program. But in my view his case for revolutionary socialism is too brief and generalized to be convincing. What remains most memorable about McLeod is the gradual, dramatic revelation of his noble character, not his basic argument. Coolly detached at the beginning of the novel, he impressively establishes himself at the end as an individual of tortured intellectual consciousness.

The real darkness of the world, of the novel itself, inheres in man, not in any government he erects. McLeod explains that "civilization" (moral decency) is necessary for the establishment of socialism. The problem, he believes, is that there are not "sufficient numbers" of decent men to create a socialist world. But so polemical does he become that it seems at times that Mailer is writing a tract. The characters of *Barbary Shore* seem to be less full-bodied creations of humanity than personifications of certain sociological tenets. Lovett alone escapes categorization, and this only because his identity is so vague. Not comprehend ing himself, he becomes incomprehensible to the reader. One accepts that Lovett does not know who he is, but he remains ambiguous because Mailer himself seems not to have a clear understanding of who Lovett is.

We can probably best understand him by comparing his passivity to the subdued nature of Albert Camus's rebellious hero Mersault in *The Stranger*. But where Camus creates a compelling portrait of alienation, Mailer does not. Lovett's predicament is never transmuted into a disturbing question. Mailer claims that *Barbary Shore* is America's first existential novel, but Lovett does not palpably engage in the primary existential act of creating his own ethical values from an unvarnished and deeply felt experience of the world.

Yet if the characterization of Lovett does not always satisfy, the book as a whole can be enjoyed. It gains in dimension if one thinks of the literary heritage from which it grew. The rooming house brings to mind the cave-like basement in Maxim Gorky's *The Lower Depths* and the squalid tavern in O'Neill's *The Iceman Cometh*. The last third of the novel, like Gorky's play, is a socialist call to action, and Hickey's confessional monologue in O'Neill's play forms an interesting parallel to McLeod's.

Generally, though, the inhabitants of Mailer's purgatorial rooming house remind one of Eliot's people existing, as they do in "The Dry Salvages," "among the breakage," each a separate "sphere of existence." How well Eliot's choric lines from *The Family Reunion* bear upon the ambience of Mailer's world:

> In an old house there is always listening, and
>   more is heard than is spoken.
> And what is spoken remains in the room, waiting
>   for the future to hear it.

> And whatever happens began in the past, and
> presses hard upon the future.

Eliot's chorus declaims that "catastrophes" have come
about because "we have lost our way in the dark."
It is the nature of that dark that *Barbary Shore*
dramatizes.

But is our national reality as grievous as Mailer
maintains? Are we ready to accept, for example, sexual
deviation (Guinivere's nymphomania, Lannie's and
Guinivere's lesbian relationship, Hollingsworth's sado-
masochism and his covert desire for McLeod) as
broadly as Mailer intends us to: that is, as a corollary
for the extreme spiritual decay of America? One
appreciates the sensitivity of his grim national portrait,
but, still, one asks if America is really such a cultural
tundra.

The vibrant portrait of Guinivere, however, seems
to compensate for any deficiencies or distortions we
may find in Mailer's social perspective. With her he
achieves what seemingly he has been trying to evoke
with the other four characters—a vivid, real-life creation. Although a slattern and a gross materialist, and
thereby a perennial type, she is the only character in
the book who generates a felt presence. Radiating an
almost Falstaffian vigor, she is so alive that she becomes both individual and type. It is perhaps because
she is so different from Lovett that she emerges so
sharply. Guinivere is brazen, touchy, touching, trifling,
pathetic, and gamey. She is bewildered and bewilder-
ing. The novel's themes of absurdity and courage
converge in her.

In conclusion, *Barbary Shore* is a book born of
much polemical thought. Thus its final effect on the
reader is of life argued rather than life lived. It will
be remembered as a unique study of a strangely
desiccated world, and also as a book that took Mailer,

like Lovett, down a dark alley. For Mailer did not
develop in this novel a sure and individualized
narrative voice. In fact, he did not do so until thirteen
years later with *An American Dream.*

4

○○○○○○○○○○○○○○○○○○○○○○○○○○○○○○○○○○○○○○

The Artist's Plight:
The Deer Park

For most people the ordered security of middle-class life is a viable alternative to the supposedly savage brutality of a man like Sergeant Sam Croft or the supposedly hopeless spiritual searching of a man like Lieutenant Robert Hearn or Michael Lovett. In his masterful short story, "The Man Who Studied Yoga," Mailer explored the cost of such an alternative.

Sam and Eleanor Slovoda live in a smartly functional apartment complex in the New York borough of Queens. They consider themselves chic but upright and congratulate themselves for holding what they deem enlightened social and political views. Sam makes a good living writing continuities for comic strips. On a Sunday evening, while the children are visiting their grandmother, the Slovodas invite two couples to their home for a small dinner party. Marvin Rossman, a dentist, brings a pornographic film, which they all guardedly watch and later discuss. "As intelligent people they must dominate it." After their guests leave, the Slovodas run the film again and make love on the couch as they watch it. Eleanor falls asleep afterward, and Sam lies awake beside her anxiously ruminating on his unrealized potentialities; he wants to write a novel; he thinks he should be conferring his sexual benefits on more women.

Mailer describes in this story the inner life of only

one character because he wants to distill and emphasize only one particular kind of sensibility: a self-conscious, second-rate man who knows and admires what distinction is but cannot attain it. The story reveals no other psyches to divert or blur Mailer's focus. The effect is that we get a small collection of flat, minor characters who heighten the portrait of Sam.

Cassius O'Shaugnessy, whom Sam's friend Sperber knew at college, is the man who studied yoga. Though he never appears and is developed only through others' comments at the party, he is the moral model of the story, the man against whom the others are measured and found lacking. A world traveler, Cassius continually experiments with his life, testing and identifying the self in relation to wide varieties of experience. Contrastingly, Sam is entrenched in bourgeois duty and domesticity. Cassius's exploratory approach to life is a critical commentary on the Slovodas and their guests, who continually try to prejudge and control experience. The suggestion is that reflection upon experience is antipodal to its enjoyment. Sperber jokes about the time Cassius entered a yoga trance in India and declared, "Damn if my ass didn't fall off." Cassius is mocking here the illusion of trying to derive meaning from life by way of a mystical state. The end point of isolated introspection is oneself, not harmony with the natural world. Though Mailer believes that the fuller the knowledge of one's underground being, the further advanced one is in the struggle to comprehend reality, he holds that this knowledge must not be passive or arrived at in isolation; rather, it must be confirmed in action.

There is also in the story a demihero—Sam's analyst, Dr. Sergius. Sam believes that the novel he longs to write will atone for the enfeebling compromises of his life and regenerate him. He feels, however, that the writing of such a novel must be predicated on the exploration of his deepest self. Sam's analyst is a giver of light, for he leads him into the darkness that illumines—the subconscious mind. He helps Sam to track down psychic promptings that have long gnawed at him but which, until now, have remained ungraspable. Dr. Sergius is an intelligent force, especially when compared to Sam's friends, who have little awareness of how to accommodate the strivings of the Freudian id to reality.

Mailer's treatment of Dr. Sergius seems affirmative, but on closer inspection he is an ambiguous character, for he has much to do with Sam's failure as an artist. The fact that Dr. Sergius has knowledge is only part of the picture; he has power as well. He leads Sam to his inner life, but he also interprets the nature of Sam's subliminal needs instead of letting Sam interpret them and act on them for himself. Once Sam is put in touch with his underground being, he acquiesces to the doctor's understanding of it. He allows a psychoanalyst's thoughts about his subconscious life to take precedence over his own.

Let it be asked then: once a man is put in touch with his subconscious life, what is to be done with it? Again, we look to Cassius. Cassius *enacts* his values. The story's theme is that no amount of rational analysis will actualize man's creative desires. Cassius's vitality and openness to experience are a result of his choosing *existence* over *thought*. The flaw in Sam's life is his lack of courage to do the same, to leap from an idea to its realization. Such a leap might appear aimless to the rational mind, but the necessity of it is born in the unconscious, which, Mailer believes, has a powerful teleological sense. Its pulsations convey to the self what is and what is not conducive to growth. The example of Cassius anticipates what is to become Mailer's central concern about man's unconscious self in all his later work. In "Hip, Hell, and the Navigator," an interview collected in *Advertisements for Myself*, Mailer said that the unconscious has "an enormous teleological sense, . . . it moves toward a goal, . . . it has a real sense of what is happening to one's being at each given moment." It sends up messages saying, "'Things are getting better' or 'Things are getting worse.'"

That man's collection of powers, urges, and appetites will create chaos in himself and in the world if unregulated by a supervisory ego is the view of established social and institutional powers. Cassius is deemed "weird" by Eleanor Slovoda and "psychopathic" by Marvin Rossman. But Mailer's view, in opposition to classical psychoanalytic theory, is that since the subconscious is self-regulating, it is the supervisory ego itself that needs controlling because it impedes the spontaneous flow of creative passions.

Ultimately, what causes Sam's pain and frustration is not his shallow social life or his intimidating wife, but his inability to express his anxiety in open revolt. Thus his freedom is only a prospect, an intense hope for tomorrow. He will continue to live out his days in quiet desperation. For Sam and millions like him, life is a horizontal fall.

Beneath Mailer's composed narrative voice lies an urgent injunction to those to whom it applies: you must drastically change your life. Like Mailer's fiction of the 1960s, this story can be read as a call to action. What Mailer means by action is bringing the intuitive life into just proportion with the cognitive life. Sam knows, as his friends do not, that they are all modern life's sad examples. Allowing their cognitive lives to expand without control, they have split themselves off from the intuitive life. "'It's all schizoid,' Sam says. 'Modern life is schizoid.'" The plight and the quest of Mailer's subsequent protagonists will be to enlarge their intuitive capabilities, to resurrect primordial energies within themselves.

"The Man Who Studied Yoga" maintains a balanced tension between satire and mellowness. With subtleness and sagacity it renders the struggle between the heat of artistic desire and man's need for the comforts of convention. In its concern with such a struggle and in its telling depiction of failed human relationships, it anticipates *The Deer Park*.

In *Advertisements for Myself*, Mailer describes *The Deer Park* as: "the painful story of two people who are strong as well as weak, corrupt as much as pure, and fail to grow despite their bravery in a poor world, because they are finally not brave enough, and so do more damage to one another than to the unjust world outside them." The story of the movie director Charles Eitel and his mistress, Elena Esposito, is told by Sergius O'Shaugnessy, a young Air Force Lieutenant. Flying regular missions over what is now North Korea, Sergius firebombed innocent people, many of whom were children and, like himself, orphans. His stark realization that the barbarity of the world is an active force within his own nature, not an alien thing outside himself, renders him sexually impotent. After the war he comes to Desert D'Or, a resort frequented by the Hollywood community (it is modeled on Palm Springs), for a rehabilitative vacation. At Desert D'Or he meets an assortment of people—stars, starlets, producers, sensualists, panderers—and moves into their sphere of influence. He is restored to potency by Lulu Meyers, a frivolous glowing sex goddess.

Eventually, with a growing awareness of his own artistic capabilities (Sergius wants to be a novelist) and with the friendship of Charles Eitel, he comes to realize that the movie stars who are America's surrogate royalty and the producers who mass-market them really make up a reverse royalty; it is not nobility but gilded ignobility that these kings and queens, dukes and duchesses, represent. At the story's end, Sergius goes to Mexico to study bullfighting and finally to New York to undertake the novel that has been germinating within him—*The Deer Park* itself. Contrastingly, Charles Eitel stays in Hollywood and helplessly watches his creative capacity decline.

Eitel is the novel's fallen hero. He has been accurately described as "Mailer's version of the traditional hero in his last historical incarnation. Vision, passion, and courage have dwindled in Eitel to intelligence, compassion, and guilt."[1] He directed brilliant films of honest social consciousness in the 1930s. But after World War II, when a Congressional investigative committee accuses him of communist involvements, he refuses to become a "friendly witness" and thereby sacrifices a glamorously successful career as one of Hollywood's top box office directors. Blacklisted by every studio, Eitel tries to revive his dormant creative powers and write a screenplay that will atone for all the slick, gaudy movies he has made since his fine early work. His inability to do so forms the central drama of the novel.

Eitel operates under the assumption that tapping into artistic energy necessarily involves the love of a woman:

. . . the core of Eitel's theory was that people had a buried nature—"the noble savage" he called it—which was changed and whipped and trained by everything in life until it was almost dead. Yet if people were lucky and if they were brave, sometimes they would find a mate with the same buried nature and that could make them happy and strong. At least relatively so.

But Sergius O'Shaugnessy operates under a different assumption: the creation of an art work involves not *loving* a woman, but *fighting* the world that is continually trying to crush the creative powers of this "noble savage." Being "happy and strong" has to do with delving into one's buried psyche, not with allying oneself, however "lucky" or "brave" that alliance may be, with a woman. It is not coincidental that Sergius begins *The Deer Park* by mentioning the prospectors who built their shanties at Desert D'Or and took to the mountains to mine for gold. Mining is Mailer's long-standing metaphor for artistic creation; the mine is the creative psyche, and the artist is the prospector.

When Eitel takes up with the sullen, beautiful Elena, he finds himself wrestling with her problems as much as with his own. She so weakens his powers that he becomes vulnerable to the ingratiations of producer Collie Munshin, a fascinating combination of venality and warmth, who offers him a lucrative contract to rewrite his screenplay to suit public taste. Eitel accepts. The result is a stylish vulgarization of his original conception. The movie is a big success and reinstates him with Herman Teppis, conspiratorial head of Supreme Pictures. Eitel becomes proficient now at playing licentious Pygmalion to talentless, dependent women and making glossy movies. His final capitulation is compliance with the Congressional investigating committee.

Despite personal defeat, Eitel nevertheless harbors an inviolate vision of what it is to grow, a vision that constitutes the moral base of the novel. Once reaccepted into the synthetic world of Hollywood, he realizes his sterile condition and reflects that "the essence of spirit . . . was to choose the thing which did not better one's position but made it more perilous." He imparts the lessons of his self-judgments to Sergius.

The Eitel-Sergius relationship is a tutor-tyro one. Eitel frankly assesses Sergius and encourages "self-

analysis." What Eitel means by self-analysis is the
creation of an art work. He believes that only in an
art work can man discover the deepest reaches of his
self and give vital form to his strivings. But Eitel's
basic weakness is that his belief is more intellectual
than emotional. Devotion to art, Mailer contends,
is a leap of faith. It is an intuitional dynamic.
Eitel *knows*, but he does not have the instinctual
sense to *act* on what he knows. Unproductive awareness is the essence of his marred dignity. His failure
makes clear his function as a sacrificial hero: he does
for others what he cannot do for himself. His middle
name, Francis, suggests a parallel with F. Scott
Fitzgerald, who also spent his last days in Hollywood
writing potboiler movie scripts.

Eitel's other pupil, Elena, learns to be more brave
than her teacher when she stands apart from him and
the forces that dishonor him. Discarded mistress of
other men, an unimpressive actress with ungainly
social manners, Elena is yet heroic in her embattled
desire to be self-reliant and take her own measure
free of men's estimation of her. Her mentality is
ordinary, her family origins plebeian; like Sergius, who
grew up in an orphanage and learned the laws of life
on the streets, she possesses great pluck. Although
assailed constantly by the barbs of fortune, she nevertheless clings to the hope of self-knowledge. She retains
her individualism when Eitel does not. More deeply
than Sergius, she learns from Eitel that "there was that
law of life so cruel and so just which demanded that
one must grow or else pay more for remaining the
same."

"Remaining the same" results from capitulation
to external power. But growth, we are led to believe,
is a self-propelling thing that culminates in creativity.

There are two principles at work in *The Deer
Park*: the principle of power and the principle of

creation. The first is Teppis's and Munshin's and has to do with providing a fantasy (the movies) into which people can escape from a world they find too harsh to bear. To maintain his power, Teppis invokes a clever strategy; he gives affection, status, and money to his stars so that they, in turn, will be dependent on him and thus compelled to obey the outworn precepts of puritan morality he sets down for them. One of the most brilliantly rendered scenes in the novel is the episode in which Teppis coerces Lulu Meyers into marriage with Teddy Pope, a homosexual movie star whose Bimmler (rating) has been dropping. Teppis's paternal scolding, Lulu's petulant resistance, and Teddy Pope's feminine fretfulness compose a portrait of perhaps the most scandalous family in American fiction, and one of the most comic.

The principle of creation concerns self-determination and, for Eitel and Sergius, the development of character. Art for them is a code of conduct. For all of *The Deer Park*'s concentration on modern mores, its ethical imperative is a rather outdated one: only sacrifice and hard work will transcend "the mummery of what happens, passes, and is gone." Eitel believes that in a society that insidiously marshals the self into patterns of conformity, the creation of art is the only strategy against anonymity. An "art work," Sergius eventually realizes through Eitel's sad example, will give him "dignity" and enable him to "keep in some permanent form those parts of myself which are better than me." Art does for Sergius what Mount Anaka did for Sam Croft in *The Naked and the Dead*; it teaches him that only through identification with impersonal beauty can human suffering and human limitation be transcended.

As for man's responsibility to society, the novel suggests that one embraces mankind by dutifully exercising one's chosen profession, not by throwing

one's arms around it. The basic connection between
the individual and society is one's work. In Sergius's
terms, the world embodied in an "art work" is the
"real world" because it is the honest and permanent
distillate of one's selfhood. Desert D'Or is the
"imaginary world" because it is devoted to that which
is corporeal—physical beauty and material success—
and therefore wholly perishable.

Yet so powerfully does this "imaginary world"
militate against man's will for self-actualization that
part of Mailer suspects that a measure of wickedness
is required to resist it. Thus he cannot wholly have
faith in Sergius, who is too nice a fellow. There is an
element of primordial demonism in Mailer's vision of
life which causes him to establish an apocalyptic
Tiresias, Marion Faye, as *The Deer Park*'s alternate
hero. The inversion of all conventional notions of
goodness, Faye is a pimp and a dope pusher. He is a
gourmet of evil, a confessor to women, a prober into
men's hearts. His "clear gray eyes" symbolize his
amorality.

Faye commits himself to the idea of noncommit-
ment. His premise is that only by being free from
responsibility to others and unbound by compassion—
"the queen to guilt"—can the self be strong and
autonomous. He tries to cut his way through the
sentimental morass of pity by refusing a groveling
dope addict money and by persuading Elena to kill
herself. But he cannot suppress his feelings. He burns
with sympathy for Paco the junkie and is relieved
when Elena ultimately refuses to commit suicide. He
fails in both cases because, for all his tough-minded-
ness, he operates under the naïve assumption that a
hard, cold will can overpower the heart.

Others call him a sadist, but he takes no real
pleasure in inflicting pain. And though he is a sexual
athlete, he takes no particular delight in sensuality.

He is unquestionably the most intriguing character in *The Deer Park*. He has phantasmagoric dreams of cosmic warfare between God and the Devil; he alone is unscathed by the conspiracies of the Hollywood hierarchy; he uses Tarot cards; he studies "odd books" in the dark hours of the morning; he is something of a warlock. But all to what end? His rampant iconoclasm is not purposive, for his primary vision is of a cleansing holocaust—the annihilation of himself and the entire earth. Yet he does not consider what should or could rise upon the ruins. We can hardly accept Faye for what Mailer intends him—a valid foil to Sergius.

Actually, Marion Faye is Mailer's first embodiment of his hipster-psychopath philosophy, a philosophy he does not cogently express until two years later in his essay "The White Negro." That Mailer surrounds his characterization of Faye with a mesh of psychological-*cum*-metaphysical pronouncements attests to his need to explain Faye's significance in expository prose.

Indeed, both Faye and Sergius are unconvincing, each for opposite reasons. Faye is developed beyond any dramatic justification, and Sergius is not developed enough. Though Mailer makes clear the moral urgency of Sergius's situation—the conflicting claims of the "imaginary world" and the "real world"—he seldom presents him reacting dramatically to it, and so the reader does not have a felt sense of involvement with Sergius. In *Advertisements for Myself*, Mailer discusses the inception of *The Deer Park* and says that for six years he had been "unable to create a narrator in the first person who was not overdelicate, oversensitive, and painfully tender." But by so purposively trying to avoid such a narrator, Mailer has given us Sergius, who is undersensitive and nearly devoid of tenderness; at least that is how he presents himself.

Sergius is offered a movie contract; he loses the love
of Lulu; he cuts loose and goes to Mexico, then to
New York. His story is one of tribulation, temptation,
renunciation, and exile. Yet so blithely does he tell us
about his *rite de passage* that we fail to feel its full
emotional import. Things happen to him without
things happening inside him.

Further, what are we to make of Sergius's relation
to sex? Led to believe throughout the novel that the
creation of art is the one redemptive experience, we are
faced in the end with Sergius's assertion that new
psychic circuits are connected through sex. Is sex or
art redemptive? And if sexuality nourishes art, how
does it do so?

Happily, what more than compensates for the
flaws in the characterization of Sergius is the brilliant
delineation of the affair between Eitel and Elena.
With scrupulous honesty Mailer renders an intensive,
intimate portrayal of a relationship—its dynamic of
sensual rapture and love, its attendant disillusionment,
its deterioration, its final stale disablement. Mailer's
two characterizations are charged with life: Eitel, the
suave but tortured gentleman whose perverse will
compels him, despite his radiant intelligence, to debase
his artistic talents; Elena, the desperate, graceless
beauty, humiliated by men and simple in her understanding of life, but valiantly in possession of self-
dignity. Sergius talks about himself with phony
tartness, but he narrates the Eitel-Elena affair with
dispassionate, muscular wisdom. As a novel about the
journey of love, *The Deer Park* has a justifiable claim
to greatness.

Reinforcing the doomed, airless quality of the
Eitel-Elena affair is the novel's setting, Desert D'Or.
It is the unifying center of the entire book, a persistent
atmospheric presence that gives palpable form to the
"prisons of pain, the wading pools of pleasure, and the

public and professional voices of our sentimental land."
This for Mailer constitutes American culture at large.
Desert D'Or is an infernal arena of "middle aged
desperados of corporation land and the suburb" locked
into a perpetual round of greed and duplicitous lust.
The desert that surrounds the resort symbolizes the
spiritual wasteland within. Windowless facades and
walled-in patios give sanctuary to people who have
relinquished their souls to Mammon and Eros. The
very word "resort" calls to mind "last resort." The
inhabitants are desperate. The town possesses no tradition or heritage or recognizable past. It is a "no-man's
land of the perpetual present." Sergius remarks on the
"air cooled midnight" of the town's bars:

Drinking in that atmosphere, I never knew whether it was
night or day . . . . afternoon was always passing into night,
and drunken nights into the dawn of a desert morning.
One seemed to leave the theatrical darkness of afternoon
for the illumination of night, and the sun of Desert D'Or
became like the stranger who the drunk imagines to be
following him.

Man has been divorced from the diurnal cycle. Symbolically, his connection with organic life has been
severed.

Mailer's purgatorial—indeed, Dantean—vision of
Desert D'Or imbues his realistic story with an epical
gravity and intensifies its moral theme enunciated by
Eitel: " 'One cannot look for a good time, Sergius, for
pleasure must end as love or cruelty'—and almost as
an afterthought, he added 'or obligation.' " *The Deer
Park* is an ironic prose elegy about people seeking
after pleasure as though it were happiness.

5

○○○○○○○○○○○○○○○○○○○○○○○○○○○○○○○○○○○○

The Writer as Outlaw:

Advertisements for Myself

In 1959, at the age of thirty-six, Mailer published a personal retrospect of his literary life. *Advertisements for Myself* is a compendium of his writings, almost all previously published, from the first eighteen years of his career. It is a multigeneric display of short stories, poems, plays, essays, articles, interviews, letters, excerpts from novels, and columns from *The Village Voice*. This assemblage is interlinked with commentary, what Mailer calls "Advertisements," in which he chronicles his fervent efforts—through honor and dishonor, security and paranoia, aspiration and disillusion, recklessness and remorse—to realize the best in himself through art. In writing openly and movingly about these struggles, Mailer comes out from behind his fiction and establishes himself as a national personality, an undeniable literary presence whose admissions recall the self-promoting strategies of Walt Whitman, that earlier oracular voice of the American experience. There is, however, an undertone of vehemence that tugs at this book from start to finish: "I have not gotten nicer as I have grown older, and I suspect that what has been true for me may be true for a good many of you."

The "Advertisements" provide Mailer with a rostrum from which he bombards the pieties, inhibitions, and banalities that seem to him to be stultifying Amer-

ican life in the 1950s and to be interfering with his own
growth as a writer. He inveighs against American society for what he deems its obsessive conformity, its
rigid sexual attitudes, its vulgar materialism, its virulent anti-communism. His primary target is "totalitarianism," the fascistic philistinism of the Eisenhower
years (1952 to 1960). Though Senator Joseph Mc-
Carthy is seldom mentioned, it seems that everywhere
his invidious ghost haunts these pages. Mailer believes
that McCarthy's inquisitorial methods of ferreting out
alleged communists and communist sympathizers from
all levels of professional life set the repressive tone for
the era. He assails right-wing America for fomenting
public hatred against the Soviet Union and for bringing the country to the edge of nuclear holocaust. Both
personally and professionally, the cold war period was
the unhappiest time of Mailer's life.

A diseased America causes Mailer to establish a
new voice. This is his first book of protest and revolt.
An example from his first "Advertisement":

The shits are killing us, even as they kill themselves—each
day a few more lies eat into the seed with which we are
born, little institutional lies from the print of newspapers,
the shock waves of television, and the sentimental cheats
of the movie screen. Little lies, but they pipe us toward
insanity as they starve our sense of the real. We have
grown up in a world more in decay than the worst of the
Roman Empire, a cowardly world chasing after a good
time (of which last one can approve) but chasing it
without the courage to pay the price of full consciousness,
and so losing pleasure in pips and squeaks of anxiety. We
want the heats of the orgy and not its murder, the
warmth of pleasure without the grip of pain, and therefore
the future threatens a nightmare, and we continue to
waste ourselves. We've cut a corner, tried to cheat the
heart of life, tried not to face our uneasy sense that
pleasure comes best to those who are brave, and now we're
a nation of drug addicts (caffeine, equanil, seconal and

nicotine), of homosexuals, hoodlums, fart-faced Southern
governors and a President so passive in his mild old panics
that women would be annoyed if one called him feminine.
The heat of our juvenile delinquency is matched only by
the unadmitted acceleration of our race into cancer, that
disease which is other than disease, that wave of undifferentiated function, the orgy of the lost cells.

Mailer may rather enjoy being embittered; he certainly must have got satisfaction from his "Advertisements" because they are written with a freedom and a
brio never before found in his work. Gone is the dispassionate, workmanlike prose so characteristic of his
previous novels and his early Farrellesque stories of
social realism. Now we get a prose of propulsive vigor,
of pungently sensuous flourishes grounded upon a
brooding earnestness. Together these "Advertisements"
form a self-inventory; they show us Mailer grimly
taking stock of himself amid a waste of broken resolves
to write a novel that would have brought to fruition
the early promise he showed at the age of twenty-five
in *The Naked and the Dead*.

I had the luck to have a large talent and to use some of
it, and I know how very well much more I could have
done if new luck had come my way, well . . . while it is
our own fault, it is not all our own fault, and so I still feel
rage at the cowardice of our time which has ground down
all of us into the mediocre compromises of what had been
once our light-filled passion to stand erect and be original.

The fourth "Advertisement" is the book's best.
With that wisdom which is woe, Mailer relates the history of his struggle to publish *The Deer Park*. He takes
the manuscript to seven publishers. Fearing possible
obscenity charges, they all reject it. Ten weeks of rejection nearly ruin him. His nervous system cannot take
it. Drinking his way through the writing of this third
novel wrecks his liver. He is exhausted. When the

eighth publisher, G. P. Putnam, finally accepts the book, his fatigue and mortification are but slightly allayed—rather, they turn to rage.

. . . something broke in me, but I do not know if it was so much a loving heart, as a cyst of the weak, the unreal, and the needy, and I was finally open to my anger. I turned within my psyche I can almost believe, for I felt something shift to murder in me. I finally had the simple sense to understand that if I wanted my work to travel further than others, the life of my talent depended on fighting a little more, and looking for help a little less. . . . All I felt then was that I was an outlaw, a psychic outlaw, and I liked it, I liked it a good night better than trying to be a gentleman . . .

Mailer now comes to realize that he must not merely take stock of himself, but take stock *in* himself. He must, he feels, have renewed faith in his own power and set himself against the world at large—its institutions, its customs, its anemic conventions—in order to realize the enormous literary ambition he proclaims for himself: to "settle for nothing less than making a revolution in the consciousness of our time." The stock responses and self-deluding moral categories that, he believes, the American public brings to art of honesty and vision lead him to the knowledge that the authentic creative life is a sustained conflict always to be fought alone. From now on Norman Mailer will exercise rather than suffer the proud man's contumely.

But first he sets a precondition for himself: to make his work "travel further than others" and write a novel that will rank with the best of the American and European masters, he must take a close look at where he has been. That is the purpose of *Advertisements for Myself*—to reflect on what he has done and clear the ground for his "big novel."

He also wants to show readers already familiar with his three novels that he is accomplished in genres

other than fiction. The book includes writing which
clearly establishes Mailer as a major man of letters:
an examination of his attitude toward homosexuality,
"The Homosexual Villain"; art criticism, "An Eye on
Picasso"; literary criticism, "Evaluations: Quick and
Expensive Comments on the Talent in the Room"; a
philosophical consideration of the dramatist Samuel
Beckett, "A Public Notice on *Waiting for Godot*"; an
evaluation of sociological thought, "David Reisman
Reconsidered"; a closely reasoned study of power politics, "The Meaning of Western Defense"; an article on
the relationship between consumerism and sexual
needs, "A Note on Comparative Pornography"; an as-
sessment of the artistic-intellectual climate in postwar
America, "Our Country and Our Culture"; a Marxist
analysis of labor and leisure in America, "From Sur-
plus Value to Mass Media."

As varied as the above topics are, one thesis undergirds them all. The mass media and political parties
dishonestly promise to deliver to Americans what they
are nervously searching for: foolproof security, whole-
sale sexual gratification, financial prosperity, and a life
free from dread; but in having such things man can
only become smaller and meaner and duller. The
thesis has a corollary: society is looking in the wrong
direction for help, for it is the artist, not the appointees
of the American state—the psychiatrist, the sociolo-
gist, the economist—who can tell us who and what we
are. But just what can be done to break through the
stifling encirclements of the Eisenhower decade Mailer
does not say—until 1957 with his impassioned essay,
"The White Negro."

'The White Negro" lies at the heart of *Advertisements for Myself*. Published originally in *Dissent*,
which describes itself as "a journal devoted to radical
ideas and the values of socialism and democracy," it
has gained enormous popularity and is probably the

most frequently anthologized essay written by a contemporary American. It represents a shift in Mailer's focus, because here for the first time he concentrates on psychical rather than social reality. He takes as his province the instinctual consciousness of the urban American Negro, who operates in accordance with subliminal needs. By replacing the imperatives of society with the vitalistic imperatives of the self, the urban black makes it impossible for institutions of social control to account for him with their own terms. This demonic rebel is for Mailer the essence of "hip" and the model for "a new breed of adventurers, urban adventurers who drifted out at night looking for action with a black man's code to fit their facts. The hipster had absorbed the existentialist synapses of the Negro, and for practical purposes could be considered a white Negro."

The hipster's response to experience is intuitive, sensuous, and violent. Mailer's radical assumption is, however, that each act of individual violence, no matter how heinous it may be, subtracts from the collective violence of the state (the liquidation of European Jews, the nuclear bombings of Japan). He was later to suggest, in his writings of the late 1960s for example, that the war in Vietnam was partly the result of our inhibitive lives. Mass private constraint, a population "starved into the attrition of conformity," can precipitate mass catastrophe. Unlike individual violence, no one supposedly is responsible for war; so, says Mailer, war becomes a socially acceptable means of expressing violence.

It is in defiance of the "collective murders of the State" that the hipster develops into a psychopath. "The strength of the psychopath is that he knows (where most of us can only guess) what is good for him and what is bad for him at exactly those instants when . . . the potentiality exists to change [or] replace

a negative and empty fear with an outward action . . ."
Mailer is saying that if violence alone will overcome
an enfeebling fear, let violence be. We might be better
off closer to death than hag-ridden by the dictates of a
conformist society or emasculated by an anesthetic
modular world.

This hipster psychopath is an existentialist in an
authentic way, for his philosophy is felt, not concep-
tualized. Informed by the writings of Jean Paul Sartre,
Mailer contends that the only value is that value which
answers one's own psychological needs. ". . . there are
no truths other than the isolated truths of what each
observer feels at each instant of his existence. . . ." To
judge or view man "from a set of standards conceived
a priori to . . . experience, standards from the past," is
to preclude his right to grow according to whatever
measure he sets for himself.

The energy with which the hipster psychopath
spurs himself on to growth is derived from a continual
search for "an orgasm more apocalyptic than the one
which preceded it. Orgasm is his therapy—he knows
at the seed of his being that good orgasm opens his
possibilities and bad orgasm imprisons him." Mailer
reverses the spirit/flesh dichotomy. It is the flesh that
gives sanction and value to the spirit, not vice versa.
Spirit derives from flesh. In the orgasmic moment the
hipster believes he can become identical with God who
is "located in the senses of the body." He predicates
the health of his spirit upon good orgasm.

Ultimately, however, "The White Negro" goes
beyond social psychology and sexology and turns out
to be Mailer's portrait of his own psyche. It is a rapt
disquisition on the creative processes of the artistic
sensibility. Significantly enough, each of Mailer's subsequent protagonists in his novels is emotionally
(though not factually) autobiographical and modeled
on the hipster delineated in this essay. The vitalizing

madness and compulsive energy that underlie *The Naked and the Dead* and *Barbary Shore* surface here.

"The White Negro," then, assays a new ground: the subconscious, the creative id. Or perhaps it can be more precisely described as the dark spring of energy in the psyche that can form new parameters of being for the individual and, Mailer suggests, for the human race. "The White Negro" signifies a turning point for Mailer, a turning away from the world toward the self for sustenance, his assumption being that, since man has disenchanted the world, only his inner life now harbors residues of enchantment.

Mailer's first fictional incarnation of the White Negro is Sergius O'Shaugnessy, the hero of his short story, "The Time of Her Time." This Sergius is the apotheosis of the Sergius in *The Deer Park*. He is now a freer individual with a rebellious wit and a firmer understanding of his capabilities. A sexual athlete and a bullfighting instructor in Greenwich Village, he has conferred his virile benefits on numerous women, but when he meets Denise Gondleman, an audacious young co-ed from New York University, his prowess is challenged:

She was a Jewish girl . . . one of those harsh alloys of a self-made bohemian from a middle-class home (her father was a hardware wholesaler), and I was remembering how her voice had irritated me each time I had seen her, an ugly New York accent with a cultured overlay. Since she was still far from formed, there had been all sorts of Lesbian hysterias in her shrieking laugh and they warred with the excess of strength, complacency and deprecation which I found in many Jewish women—a sort of "Ech" of disgust at the romantic and mysterious All.

In the end, after engaging in a veritable decathlon of sexual intercourse with Denise over a period of days, Sergius manages to bring her, for the first time in her life, to a climax. But the next morning she is insolent to him for sodomizing her the night before. Her parting words are: "He [her psychoanalyst] told me your whole life is a lie, and you do nothing but run away from the homosexual that is you." Sergius admires her pluck and smilingly regrets losing her. ". . . like a real killer, she did not look back, and was out the door before I could rise to tell her that she was a hero fit for me."

"The Time of Her Time" seems outlandish, a *grand bouffe* of sexual gourmandizing. But if we understand the cultural atmosphere in which it was written, it appears to be more than just an inflated cock-and-bull story. It is, in fact, a satiric attack on the bromidic psychology of the 1950s. People like Denise Gondleman and everyone obsessed with "mental health" were in therapy and psychoanalyzing everyone else. Cheerful acceptance of one's culturally ascribed role was the key to the charmed house of adjustment. These were the days when Virginia Woolf was frowned upon for her feminism. She had a psychological problem: she could not accept being a woman. Therapists were telling people that good sex was to be derived from loving tenderness and patient caring. People were preaching the gospel of being "normal" and having "healthy relationships." If such cant annoys us, it must have made Mailer curdle. In "The Time of Her Time" his bile turns into something wild and funny.

Advertisements for Myself is an amalgam of the three themes that have always been and still are basic to Mailer's work: the individual in conflict with society, the role of the artist in the modern world, and the nature of the sexual experience. As Mailer treats them, these three themes have the same intention: to delineate the conditions of our social, psychological, and natural existence, and to show in what ways they are at odds.

It is, however, the theme of the artist in the modern world that is central to *Advertisements for Myself*. For essentially what one comes away with after reading this book is an experiential sense of what it was to be a writer in America at midcentury and, by extension, what it is to be a man. For Mailer intends us to conclude that the artist's plight is an intensification or clarification of the plight of every thinking man. What has happened to Mailer has happened to most of us. "Yes, I wanted to say, my creative rage is being sapped, I have been dying a little these fifteen years, and so have a good many of you, no doubt—none of us are doing quite so much as we once thought we would." Mailer's embitterments and hopes are ours. "I've . . . picked up too slowly on the hard, grim, and maybe manly knowledge that if I am to go on . . . , I must get better at overriding the indifference which comes from the snobs, arbiters, managers, and conforming maniacs who manipulate most of the world of letters . . ."

The probing intelligence that Mailer brings to his understanding of American culture and the artist's place within it makes *Advertisements for Myself* the most distinguished autobiography of an American writer since *The Education of Henry Adams* fifty-two years earlier. But unlike Adams, the frustrated classicist, Mailer imagines himself an artist in the traditional romantic sense; he must, he feels, break through and away from the substantial concerns of life in the workaday world. He hopes to, as critic Roy Harvey Pearce says of the poets of the American Renaissance, "*transform* himself in the breaking." It is not, in Pearce's words, "recovery and reconstitution" that romantic artists want, but "an infinite series of willed, self-generated transformations forward; the opportunity for each transformation was only that—an opportunity, its possibilities exhausted as soon as the transformation had occurred. Thus their insistent anti-formalism and their 'organicism.' "[1]

The various pieces of *Advertisements for Myself* are Mailer's series of willed, self-generated transformations forward. The book is a seedbed of the art that is to flower later. The lavish style and apocalyptic mood of his stories of the late fifties, like "The Time of Her Time," anticipate *An American Dream*. The political polemic of his essays, the social realism of his early stories, and the candid autobiography of the "Advertisements" will merge to form *The Armies of the Night*.

6

oooooooooooooooooooooooooooooooooooo

The New Hero:
An American Dream

An American Dream is about the dissolution of the self. The story, told by Stephen Richards Rojack—professor of existential psychology, author, television talk show host, ex-congressman, war hero, and general man-about-town—is the testimony of thirty-two heated, delirious hours in his life in which he casts off his old identities and perilously struggles toward psychical rebirth.

On a superficial level this novel, or pop novel, is a gothicized crime thriller that openly evokes the libidinal dimension of the collective American mind. The pivot of the book's action is Rojack's murder of his shrewish, estranged wife, Deborah Caughlin Mangaravidi Kelly, who has come to represent for him an oppressive anti-life force. Unable to endure her taunts any longer, he strangles her in her plush Park Avenue apartment, pushes her off the balcony to the busy street below, and tells the police she has committed suicide. The murder of his wife launches him into a gamut of events—at once dreadful, galvanizing, and redemptive —that take him into the wicked heartlands of New York City. With Ruta, his wife's tough German maid, he engages in a demonic bout of sodomy. He successfully resists the interrogative pressures of the police; he throttles a murderous black hipster, Shago Martin; he wrests himself free from the satanic coils of his

father-in-law, Barney Oswald Kelly, a man of indeter-
minate wealth and power. His adventures even lead
him to love with a soiled yet pure cabaret singer,
Cherry Melanie. When she is pointlessly killed, Rojack
sets out for the primal realm, the prehistoric jungles of
Yucatán and Guatemala.

Mailer intends this novel to be a fiery chisel working its way into all the dull lairs of American guilt
and malaise. His method is to present a narrator whose
senses are unsheathed, who looks at the world—indeed, smells it, feels it, hears it, tastes it—with an
accelerated consciousness. In a recent interview in
Partisan Review, Mailer describes Rojack's condition:
"He's in an incandescent state of huge paranoia and
enormous awareness. He's more heroic and more filled
with dread than at any point in his life. So he comes
in like a lighthouse in a fog."[1] Rojack is a man operat-
ing on an edge between life and death, for at the
dramatic heart of the novel is the conflict between creative and destructive power.

The principal theme of the novel argues, however,
for intimacy with destruction, not separation from it.
The symbolic projection of this theme is Rojack's walk
on Barney Kelly's parapet. When Kelly hears of his
daughter's death, he summons Rojack to his luxuriously
sinister apartment high atop the Waldorf Towers. The
two men meet in mutual suspicion. Waves of violence
waft off Kelly. An impulse wells up in Rojack, a voice
from his inner monitor: to extricate himself from Kelly,
whom he envisions as the Devil's viceroy, he must go
to the terrace and walk the parapet. With quaking
heart, he circles the parapet, peering into the black
abyss below. When he completes his walk, Kelly tries
to push him off. Rojack resists his prod and jumps
safely back to the terrace.

To court death and thus gain an intensification of
life is an existential tactic Mailer has learned from

Ernest Hemingway. An instinctual logic that is particularly Mailer's informs this tactic: in order to realize our potential, the overlay of societal conformity that insulates the mind must be actively broken through by taking risks, by pushing ourselves, if necessary, to the limits of experience. Triumph over the modern maladies of fragmentation, chaos, and dismay can only be effected by meeting them head on. Facing into the dread means for Mailer the possibility of destroying stale conceptual modes and of forging new synapses, new circuits of energy. The parapet experience is the metaphoric dramatization of his philosophy of self-renewal.

Mailer expresses the conflict of the creative and destructive elements of existence through a whole pattern of symbolic antinomies: vagina/anus, soul/cancer, Central America/New York, God/Devil, instinct/society. Transcending these antinomies is the central symbol of the book—the moon, which represents truth or being. Throughout the novel it functions as a catalytic agent conveying telepathic messages to Rojack which he can only vaguely understand but which endow him with divine magic and urge him in the direction of psychical growth. It was the moon that gave him the ability in World War II to singlehandedly attack and kill four Germans in a machine gun nest. As a result, he was awarded the Distinguished Service Cross and an open door to a Congressional seat. It is the moon that prompts him to strangle Deborah and later walk around Kelly's parapet. But Rojack is not always brave enough to follow the moon's messages. When it counsels him to circle the parapet one more time for Cherry, his nerve fails. He flees to her apartment only to find her murdered by a Harlem thug who mistakenly believed she plotted the death of her former lover, Shago Martin. In failing to obey the moon, Rojack fails Cherry. And he fails the moon itself.

The Creation is affected by what man does because, as Mailer writes in his notice on Samuel Beckett's
play, *Waiting for Godot* (*Advertisements for Myself*),
"God's destiny is flesh and blood with ours." The
aridity of the moon is symbolic of the fears that cripple
growth. But this aridity can be transmuted into vital
life, Mailer maintains, by acts of courage. When the
moon whispers its promptings to Rojack, it is endeavoring to renew itself. The cosmos can improve if Rojack
acts bravely. Such is the mythical meaning Mailer
attributes to Rojack. As man acts with courage or
cowardice, as he chooses experiment or convention,
so he advances or impedes the evolutionary process
of the cosmos. Man is a living line of purpose born
of eternity.

Mailer's God is most unchurchly, however, for He
is not omnipotent. Like man himself, He is struggling
for completion in the existential sense of making Himself. Far from having a bit part in the cosmic drama,
man is the embodiment or instrument of God's endeavor to grow. And it may happen, as Mailer suggests
in this novel, that God will enlist man to help Him in
His ongoing battle with the Devil, thereby impelling
man beyond his natural limits. How robust and ecstatic
a vision this is with which Mailer refutes the current
literary image of man as a sadly laughable creature
caught up in a network of circumstances beyond his
power to know or control. Rojack trembles. He falters.
But always he feels that the fact of his being alive is
not arbitrary happenstance. He has been launched
into the world by a power greater than himself, and
it is his purpose to help actualize that power through
the exertions of his own creative will.

Mailer's vision of Rojack emerges from his understanding of the psychopathic hipster formulated seven
years before in "The White Negro":

the decision [of the hipster] is to encourage the psychopath in oneself, to explore that domain of experience where security is boredom and therefore sickness, and one exists in the present, in that enormous present which is without past or future, memory or planned intention, the life where a man must go until he is beat, where he must gamble with his energies through all those small or large crises of courage and unforeseen situations which beset his day, where he must be with it or doomed not to swing. The unstated essence of Hip, its psychopathic brilliance, quivers with the knowledge that new kinds of victories increase one's power for new kinds of perception; and defeats, the wrong kind of defeats, attack the body and imprison one's energy until one is jailed in the prison air of other people's habits, . . . defeats, boredom, quiet desperation, and muted icy self-destroying rage.

Rojack is the new primitive. An intellectual attuned to his nonrational being, a cultured savage, he is the type of man who, Mailer hopes, will someday emerge in America to thrive beyond the repressions of the state. Mailer invites us to understand *An American Dream* as an evolutionary novel and suggests, paradoxically, that Rojack evolves by going back—back, that is, to his primordial being. The way up is the way down. The subconscious, Mailer still believes, is the mind of primordial being. It is an energy, an intelligence, existing outside time and civilization. Rojack's primary commitment is to understand this mysterious mental region, to learn the face of the deep, and then to act eventfully in the world to substantiate his newfound knowledge.

One may well ask, "What good can come from the deliberate cultivation of subconscious needs? Does not this amount to insanity?" Mailer would agree that it does. But always the suggestive thrust of his writings has been that insanity is unavoidable in contemporary America. That which social tradition deems sanity, he argues, is actually sickness: the military (*The Naked and the Dead*); political parties (*Barbary Shore*); and show business (*The Deer Park*). For Mailer the social realities of our time offer a grim proposition: one's choice is not between sanity and insanity, but between static insanity and creative insanity, or what he calls "psychopathy." The theme of *An American Dream* is the clarification and intensification of the subconscious self. It is about exhuming one's primeval being so that it can invigorate and inform the conscious mind and be brought to bear upon the social and institutional arenas of contemporary America.

The institutions in *An American Dream* are presented allegorically through certain minor characters. Rojack's television producer personifies the Corporation. His psychology department chairman, Fred Tharchman, embodies Academia. Detective Roberts represents the Law. What uniformly characterizes these institutional realms is their submission to social dictates and political force. Rojack's producer and chairman ostracize him because his wife's allegedly suicidal death is socially heinous. And Lieutenant Roberts, who from the beginning suspects Rojack of murdering his wife, stops his investigation because of vague pressure brought to bear on the New York City police department by Barney Kelly, who does not want to be under public scrutiny. The compulsive fear that dwells in American institutions is a malignant force that threatens Rojack at every turn. His strategy against it, after nine debilitating years of marriage, is to retrieve love and enter the sphere of natural being that Cherry provides.

With Cherry Rojack can abandon the roles of TV talk-show host, psychology professor, and criminal suspect—all of which pin him within an institution—and accept the mortifications of his own life. In order to gain her love, however, Rojack must plunge into an ordeal of mythological import. He descends into the underworld, the cellar nightclub of Toni Ganucci (mafioso boss in the employ of Kelly). He wrests Cherry from Ganucci and his cronies, the monster guardians, and ascends with her into the upper world. (In Greek mythology the poet Orpheus descends into Hades to rescue his beloved Eurydice.) They make love, proclaiming their resistance to denaturing technology—for Mailer the handmaiden to the institution—by discarding her diaphragm and conceiving a child.

I . . . felt her will dissolve into tears, and some great deep sorrow like roses drowned in the salt of the sea came flooding from her womb and washed into me like a sweet honey of balm for all the bitter sores of my soul and for the first time in my life without passing through fire or straining the stones of my will, I came up from my body rather than down from my mind, I could not stop, some shield broke in me, bliss, and the honey she had given me I could only give back, all sweets to her womb . . .

Rojack achieves with Cherry a religiosexual consummation. His feeling for her cannot be called romantic; for in realizing his quest for escape from the pall of death, it becomes essential for him to keep the experience impersonal in order to maintain its extreme intensity. His union with Cherry is a dream-ridden act of drunkenness or half-asleep love, in which guilt and obligation are slyly avoided and "that quiver of jeweled arrows, that heavenly city" appears.

When Rojack loses Cherry, he is reminded of how inchoate his newly gained powers are. Feeling compelled to go even deeper into the primordial darkness from which he has gained what powers he has so far exerted in his struggle toward re-creating himself, he heads for the sacred domain of Yucatán and Guatemala. Rojack's old self has indeed been destroyed, but

the destruction has been vital because it is the necessary preamble to construction. His dark night of the
soul has been as traumatic as the experience of a blind
man gaining sight. He closes his narrative in dismay,
yes, but accompanying the dismay is his knowledge
that he has opened himself to immense possibilities.
Exactly because he is cut off from security and re-
spectability, he values whatever in life is new and
adventurous. *An American Dream* is a book that rejects
conservatism in favor of radicalism for no political
reason but because conservatism is order and radicalism is disorder. It suggests that if life is chaotic, it
is for that very reason intense; further, the order that
is wrought out of the chaotic life is one's own. Conservatism Mailer equates with order from the outside,
from authority.

To any reader who accepts the terms of Mailer's
vision, this book generates intoxicating hope, for
Rojack is a pioneer of the spirit; his explorations give
us a felt sense of expanding possibilities for the self.
Mailer has defined character in this novel as an endless
series of second chances. His hero is trying to do what
the classic American heroes of James Fenimore Cooper
and Herman Melville tried to do before him—get away
from the enfeeblements of civilization, the crush of
history.

To give form to this struggle for unencumbered
selfhood, Mailer has fashioned a large-motioned, poly-
phonic prose of remarkable metaphoric richness. His
language is at once energetic, convolute, and lush. It
is an orchestration of gusts and magniloquent musings,
exhibiting always a quivering awareness of the tangible
world. Indeed, there are those critics who view Mailer's
style as the very *raison d'être* of the book. Treating
lightly the philosophical and sexual meaning of Rojack's plight, they have focused instead on the artistic
virtues of his language: "What matters is that he

[Rojack] makes us feel his associations as spontaneous, irresistible fantasies, and that we accept his most elaborate verbal constructions as illustrating the elaborateness of immediacy rather than of development toward an idea."[2] "What saves the book is a commitment to creativity invested not in sexual acts but in acts of writing, and not even on every page, of course, but on many of them."[3]

But it is on the very matter of style that some critics fault *An American Dream.*[4] They call attention to the book's frequent lapses of idiom. Cherry, they claim, speaks in a manner far too stilted for her social station, and Rojack's adversaries—Deborah, Kelly, Shago Martin—are intended to convey dread but all too often sound just plain silly. These criticisms of style seem to me rather off the point. After all, Rojack narrates this story and naturally from time to time imbues other characters' speech with his own verbal colors. Also, Mailer may be purposively providing his characters with certain linguistic quirks to indicate their complexity and thereby to foil our pat expectations of them. In fact, the poetic effusiveness of *An American Dream* would suggest that we are dealing with a self-delighting fabulist playing with the possibilities of language, not with a brooding realist carefully recording real-life speech. It is unfair, it seems to me, to bring to bear on such a book the criteria of realism. *An American Dream* signifies a radical departure from Mailer's earlier novels that were written in the realistic mode. The role of literature for him now becomes one of mystic release and revelation. He found in this book a way to give the immediacy of direct sensation to the morbid or sensuous dream. Areas of our nature usually left unexplored—Mailer would say untapped—are revealed.

To judge *An American Dream* by its formal attributes—which is to say its exuberant, opulent style and its breathlessly paced plot—is to rank it among the finest of contemporary American novels. But it does not favorably lend itself to consideration on an ethical level. How does Mailer justify the fact that other people have to be victimized so that Rojack can achieve rebirth? I find it difficult to sympathize with Rojack when he strives to assert himself by murder and cruelty. Of course, there is the argument that the murder of Deborah and the beating of Shago Martin are *symbolic* methods of self-renewal. What then would be the real and literal methods? Mailer does not say. And why should these symbolic methods be so sensationalistic? If we accept Mailer's essential assumption that, in one critic's words, ours is a "psychotic world bordering an apocalypse and yearning toward death," we could conceivably justify Rojack's actions as viable strategies for survival.[5] But such is not the experience of the world for most of us. Insofar as it is fair to judge literature on moral as well as aesthetic grounds, the novel suffers from its refusal to deal with the ethical nature of man's relation to man.

7

○○○○○○○○○○○○○○○○○○○○○○○○○○○○○○○○○○○

An Alaskan Odyssey:
Why Are We in Vietnam?

To read Mailer's fifth and most recent novel, *Why Are We in Vietnam?* is to imagine William Burroughs seizing upon Faulkner's story *The Bear* and having his wildly witty way with it. Rusty Jethro, a rich Texas executive, goes on an Alaskan safari to hunt grizzly bear. He hires Big Luke Fellinka, an illustrious guide and big-game hunter, to lead the way. Rusty brings two adolescent knaves with him—his son D. J., who narrates the novel, and Tex Hyde, D. J.'s neo-nazi, half-Indian buddy. Backing up Rusty's hopes and boasts every step of the way are two junior executives, Medium Asshole Bill and Medium Asshole Pete. To prove his manhood and enhance his professional status in his corporation, Rusty monomaniacally desires to shoot a "grizzer." And Big Luke, a vulgarized Daniel Boone eager for a fat remuneration, is wholly willing to oblige. He takes the hunting party up in a helicopter that flushes out of the wilderness not only grizzlies but wolf, Dall ram, and caribou. Laden with guns powerful enough to drop an elephant, the huntsmen engage in a grotesquely sporting holiday of blood.

When D. J. eventually manages to kill a bear independently without the aid of "technological infiltration," Rusty claims the bear for his own. "Whew," says D. J. "Final end of love of one son for one father." Renouncing the venality of the hunt, D. J. and Tex

set out together for the pure, mysterious wilds of the
Brooks Range above the Arctic Circle where, exultant
in their new-found freedom, they feel connected to the
extrasensory circuits of the cosmos. Bedding down at
night beneath the clear, starry firmament, they are
homoerotically drawn toward each other, while, at
the same time, fired with an impulse to kill each other.
And then the revelation: "something in the radiance
of the North went into them, . . . and they were twins,
never to be lovers again, but killer brothers, owned
by something, prince of darkness, lord of light, they
did not know." God reveals Himself to them as a
beast of "giant jaw and cavernous mouth" and says,
"Go out and kill—fulfill my will, go and kill." D. J.
and Tex join the army, and the novel ends with D. J.'s
urgent declaration, "Vietnam, hot damn."

The parable is clear. The hunting party is the
American military in miniature, replete with com-
manders and their GI subordinates. The crazed ani-
mals being annihilated by aerial machines are the
people of Vietnam napalmed by the Air Force. But
such pat equations do little to help us understand the
art or the real ideational power of this book.

It is the character of D. J.'s voice that carries all
of the novel's thematic, symbolic, and structural
weight. "Grassed out" on marijuana at his parents'
Dallas mansion and enjoying a farewell party for himself and Tex—they will be inducted into the army
the next day—D. J. narrates the events of this Alaskan
odyssey in a punning prose that is a dazzling collage
of speech from almost every arena of American life.
In rapid-fire shifts, he speaks the language of an urban
black, a pedantic psychoanalyst, a corporate bureau-
crat, a Southern redneck, a revivalist preacher, an
academic philosopher, a physicist, a McLuhanite
media critic. The impression we get is of a jammed
radio receiver picking up from multiple wavelengths

all the ideologies, buried fantasies, fears, and desires of the collective American psyche and transmitting them across the land. D. J. calls himself "Disc Jockey to the world." He is telepathically tuned in to the rumblings, the groanings, the screams and palpitations of our subterranean selves; and his voice, he imagines, is a "tape being made for the private ear of the Lord," Who will register it in His Univac-like celestial archives. D. J. is the recording secretary of our repressed compulsions—our dreams of power, our ecstatic sexual hopes, our hatreds and bigotries.

We cannot be sure, however, of D. J.'s real identity, for he is caught up in a "mystery that can't be solved . . . I'm the center of it and I don't comprehend, not necessarily, I could be traducing myself." He proposes that the source of his outrageous "stream of conch" dithyramb could be a crippled, bedridden, Harlem "spade" hallucinating that he is a rich Texas WASP. Or his narrative could be the "unwindings and unravelings of a nervous constellation just now executed."

The importance to this book of an undetermined narrator is that we are impelled to concentrate on voice rather than character, on what consciousness is doing rather than on where it comes from. D. J.'s consciousness is in the throes of trying to rid itself of that which has glutted it—namely "mixed shit," Mailer's collective symbol for all the slogans, categories, and presumptions of popular American culture. The novel is not, then, intended to be in any significant sense a study of character, because it assumes that individual character is not a viable possibility in a world where the mind control techniques of the mass media have homogenized human thought and the value of human productivity is measured by such impersonal forces as government, business, and industry. D. J.'s consciousness has been maimed and made dizzily manic by excessive input. What particularly engorges his mind are thoughts of violence, the violence that historically has been so large and pervasive a part of our national character that it is eventually exported to Southeast Asia. The energetic onrush of the tale D. J. tells may be interpreted as his attempt to purge himself of his psychic overload.

His method of release is obscenity grounded on scatological and fornicatory imagery, the immediate effect of which—bold, uproarious comedy—at first veils Mailer's philosophic intent. Feces and copulation symbolize, respectively, debilitating dread and regenerative energy. They are the metaphoric keys to Mailer's eschatology. Feces represent defeat and death. They are associated in Mailer's mind with the Devil, whose cosmic intent is to besmirch everything constructive that man does. The war God wages with the Devil is advanced on His behalf every time man engages in orgasmic copulation. This idea is first explored ten years earlier in "The White Negro." Copulation connotes for Mailer the ultimate expression of creative life because in the orgasmic moment the self psychomystically links itself to God. Anus and phallus: apocalyptic routes to damnation or salvation.

In his laudatory review of the novel, critic John Aldridge explains the moral value of Mailer's virulent obscenity. Scatological obscenity is "a means of clearing the psychic bowels of defeat and dread," a way of "ridding ourselves of the blocked aggressions, the spiritual constipations, which goad us even as they inhibit our powers of creative self-rejuvenation."[1] The social import of obscenity is that it

may also be a means of renewing vital contact between those portions of the population who habitually and at grave peril to themselves repress their aggressive impulses, and those to whom obscenity is part of the accepted vernacular language and thus constitutes a natural and healthy mode of release for those impulses. Ideally, the function of obscenity would be to mediate between the superego and the id elements of American society, releasing the buried fears and hatreds of the WASP Establishment classes to something like the emotional freedom of the Negro and hipster.[2]

D. J.'s parents represent the epitome of what Mailer deems anal-compulsive WASP anxiety. Hallie Jethro, adamantly intent on maintaining her status as a charming society matron, has so long kept desire and hate secretly locked within herself that they have turned into fantastical lusts and inflamed bigotries. In a pathetic attempt to restore her health, she goes to a flatulent psychoanalyst, Dr. Leonard Levin Fichte Rothenberg. Rusty Jethro, in order to rise in the ranks of the corporate hierarchy, has for twenty years had to do "all the little things body did not want to do." Now he is a pent-up bundle of hysterias. He heads the division of his corporation that manufactures carcinogenic cigarette filters. And cancer to Mailer means constraint. The cells proliferate, he reasons, when the individual fails to perform an outward action that will propel him toward growth. Cancer is implosion. It is, quite literally, Rusty's stock-in-trade.

Conditioned by Central Consolidated Chemical and Plastic—by its lessons of one-upmanship, its methods of social control—Rusty is oblivious to energy as creation; he knows energy only as power. The irony of his situation is, however, that in exerting power he has no sense of growth, because he does not actually possess power; he is merely its conduit. Power comes from Central Consolidated; Rusty is only the passive receiver and dispenser of this power. Mailer intends us to understand that energy as power, unlike energy as creation, springs from institutional sources, from a realm, in other words, outside the self.

D. J.'s metaphor for the corporation is the "diode,"

a valvular device that allows electrical energy to pass
through it uni-directionally. The corporation, in this
sense, represents an anticreative force because creation is born—and Mailer is not the first artist to
concede this—of inner flux between such polarities
as mind/heart, spirit/body, truth/beauty. Corporate
power, then, is static, not dynamic. It stymies all creative phenomena, love for example: ". . . love is dialectic, man, back and forth, hate and sweet, leer-love,
spit-tickle, bite-lick, love is dialectic, and corporation
is DC, direct current, diehard charge, no dialectic
man, just one-way street, they don't call it Washington, D.C. for nothing. . . ." The corporation is always
trying to stop oscillation. Indeterminancy is its bug-
bear. The exhaustively elaborate detailing of rifle
specifications in chapter five is Mailer's parody of the
rational corporate mind that cannot engage in reality
without categorizing. Rusty, Bill, and Pete cannot see
without a name.

While Rusty seeks to control the natural realm
the way Central Consolidated has controlled him, and
render it intelligible to his will by reducing its wild-
life to carnage, D. J. and Tex depart for the inviolate
snow fields of the Brooks Range. Once there they
ritualize their severance from the corporate-industrial
matrix by relinquishing their guns, knives, and com-
pass, thus symbolically cleansing themselves, they
believe, of all the "mixed shit" D. J. has been picking
up from a contaminated America. His prose is now
decontaminated. All jived-up disc-jockey jabberwocky
disappears, and his voice flows forth in beautiful legato
rhythms. D. J. changes from *poète maudit* to *plein air*
poet. The boys behold the mountains cloaked in snow,
the prismatic fields of ice, the land "white as a sheet"
as sublime affirmations of purgation and purity.
Breathlessly they observe a stalking wolf, and later
they see a great grizzly bear run down a caribou calf

and eat it. The primitive and unutterable strangeness of the world rises up to face them across the millennia. D. J. and Tex surrender themselves to the sacerdotal wilderness.

But Mailer lifts us up only to drop us down. The air of the Brooks Range is so pure, the peaks so encrusted with ice, that the mountains act as mammoth crystal sets and pick up, in the form of electro-magnetic waves, all the cowardices, devilish hankerings, and visions of power emanating from the underside of the American character—from its fantasy life. These waves collect in the Arctic and throw off rays of awe and dread, the aurora borealis for example. D. J. and Tex get caught up in a field of these reverberating waves and are defiled by them. The boys keep receiving messages from Mr. Sender—a demiurgic, unseen power broker who presides over all of institutional America—and their creative wills are confounded. In a confusion of dual energies—energy as copulation (divine strength) and energy as buggery (diabolic strength)—they are sexually impelled toward each other. But each is ready to murder the other should an advance be made. The horrific enchantment is broken when God suddenly appears as a ferocious beast. This revelation signifies to the boys that their murderous desires are ordained by nature itself. D. J. and Tex, turning their destructive hate away from themselves and toward the world at large, return home to join the army. Next stop, Vietnam!

What are we to make of such grotesquerie? It is Mailer's means of exploding the whole Adamic tradition of American literature. *Why Are We in Vienam?* is a deliberate rebuttal of the revered notion that if man removes himself from the corruptness of civilization and enters the realm of unspoiled nature, he can revive within himself something of the purity of heart and nobility of spirit that Adam must have felt in that

first world that God set specially before him. While
Mailer believes that man does indeed divorce himself
from the mystical harmonies of nature, greedily ravage
it, build war machines, decimate his own kind, and
seem generally to sing a ghastly paean to death, he
clearly suggests, by way of D. J.'s and Tex's Arctic
experience, that the origin of man's barbarity is nature
itself. Evil was in nature before it was in man. Such
is Mailer's premise, and he shares it with William
Burroughs, whose novel, *Naked Lunch*, inspired this
one. "America is not a young land: it is old and dirty
and evil before the settlers, before the Indians. The
evil is there waiting."[3] Man's iniquity is of nature.
Traditonal notions of a serene pastoralism, of a virgin
land, are for Mailer—tough-minded urbanite that he
is—nostalgic inventions of a primitive past that never
was. I will be savage, D. J. seems to be saying, because
I recognize that civilization is but another of savagery's
masks, not an enlightened journey out of darkness.

The cultural contradictions of *Why Are We in
Vietnam?*—the individual versus the corporation, inde-
pendent thought versus the electronic media—are left
unresolved because Mailer is inspired in this book by
the impulse to escape from culture itself into a realm
where nature is (in the words of critic Richard Chase
on Fenimore Cooper):

. . . terrible, and beautiful, where human virtues are
personal, alien, and renunciatory, and where contradictions
are to be resolved only by death, the ceaseless, brooding
presence of which endows with an unspeakable beauty
every irreconcilable of experience and all the irrationalities
of life.[4]

Ultimately, however, the real achievement of this
novel has more to do with the *re-creation* of cultural
contradictions than with *escape* from them; for the
greater part of D. J.'s narrative is a verbal prism of

the dire divisions within American society. To see how he renders such divisions, let us look at just one passage among many. Early in the novel, speaking in urban black vernacular, D. J. describes a Southern white menacingly interrogating a country Negro. "Whitey the Green Eye" has a nose "red as lobster . . . a-hovering and a-plunging like a Claw, man . . ." The narrative then modulates to the patter of a white, drug-ridden hipster ("ex-acid is my head, Love iS Death, . . . it's square to be frantic . . ." Then it shifts to the voice of an ingratiating "true-blue Wasp-ass" Texan extending a down-home Southern hospitality invitation to Jesus to "come visit." Here is capitalism trying to make its peace with Christianity. Interwoven in the passage are two threads. One is a brief excerpt from "In the Cool, Cool, Cool of the Evening," a popular song about the idyllic amicability of provincial American life. Another is a pun, "sick with the tick," which refers to time and the parasitic insect, both destroyers of life—thus D. J.'s query, "oh blood how rot is thy sting?" (a variation of the biblical line). Encapsulated here on half a page are the hatreds and fears, delusions and dreams, weltering within American society.

The novel is a digest of verbal parodies. Nowhere else in postwar American fiction do we see the contradictions of American culture so richly and variously voiced. We can read this novel as an oratorio for many voices, each one of which infuriates, stupefies, or fills us with dark laughter. By re-creating the duplicities and tensions that infect the American character, Mailer enables us to understand, perhaps more clearly than heretofore, why we were in Vietnam.

But, further, just as the value of the book is that it enlarges perceptions rather than offers solutions, so the moral of the book is artistic, not ideological. The medium is the message. Style, the very act of writing

itself—of release in the form of expressive invention—
is the one strategy Mailer invokes against the numbing
effects of the mass media and the "communication
engineers" of a programmed society. By mimicking the
languages of the land, he helps us to better see through
them and thereby resist their beguilements and coer-
cions. Verbal play is restorative, a spiritual tonic.
Mailer suggests it is the last physical liberty.

The book's style is complex, a kaleidoscopic burlesque of the way business executives, electrical engineers, Southerners, hipsters, blacks, and doctors talk—
and think. "I say create complexities," says Mailer in
"An Impolite Interview" (*The Presidential Papers*),
"let art deepen sophistication, let complexities be
demonstrated to our leaders, let us try to make *them*
more complex. That is a manly activity." It is an
activity which can, he asserts, diminish the totalitarian
forces of government, business, and mass communication that simplify life and brutalize man's mind by
expunging ambiguity and diversity. Rusty Jethro is
an example of what totalitarianism can do to the mind.
He thinks in determined patterns: "The women are
free. . . . The niggers are free, . . . The yellow races
are breaking loose. . . . The adolescents are breaking
loose including his own son. . . . Communism is going
to defeat capitalism, unless promptly destroyed. . . .
Church is out, LSD is in. . . ." His mind has coagulated.

A style crackling with disparate images—a style
like D. J.'s—may be, Mailer hopes, the force to fight
the progressive collectivism of our lives. In "An Impolite Interview" he says: "Art is a force. Maybe it's
the last force to stand against urban renewal, mental
hygiene, the wave of the waveless future." *Why Are
We in Vietnam?* is a brilliant sea of linguistic waves,
a book that will not hold still to be categorized, for
its intention is to subvert all category. It is a work
of anarchic but creative flux.

8

○○○

History into Art:
The Armies of the Night,
Miami and the Siege of Chicago,
Of a Fire on the Moon

In the fall of 1967 American society seemed to be coming unglued. Across the nation a massive "peace" movement was mounting against United States involvement in the Southeast Asia war. Antiwar protesters were burning their draft-cards, picketing draft-induction centers, clashing with police over the presence of military recruiters on college campuses, and hiking prayerfully through suburban streets on long peace vigils. At the University of Wisconsin at Madison, 2500 demonstrators skirmished with police over the right of Dow Chemical Corporation—which at the time manufactured napalm—to recruit job applicants on university property.

On October 21 in Washington, D.C., the antiwar movement erupted with unprecedented force. Under the tenuous direction of the New York-based National Mobilization Committee to End the War in Vietnam, forty to fifty thousand chanting, determined demonstrators—college students, hippies, hard-core revolutionaries, bogus revolutionaries, pacifists, motorcycle gangs, professionals, housewives, artists—gathered at the Lincoln Memorial and marched on to the Pentagon to close it down. An array of federal marshals and military police stood ready to quell them. Several demonstrators goaded the soldiers with the ugliest

personal slanders they could think of. Some threw
bottles and tomatoes. Others wielded clubs and ax
handles. An assault squad breached security lines,
hurling themselves, amid a fog of tear-gas, against
flailing truncheons and rifle butts. When the march
ended, one thousand demonstrators had been arrested
and dozens injured. The Pentagon remained stolid and
undefiled.

   *The Armies of the Night: History as a Novel, the
Novel as History* is an on-the-spot account of the
Pentagon march. The book is novelistic because it
sensitively describes the *effects* of the march on a
participant-protagonist, Norman Mailer, and historical
because it scrupulously describes the *facts* of the
march. Let us begin, however, with an outline of the
book's action. At his home in Brooklyn Heights, Mailer
receives a phone call from Mitch Goodman, an old
friend, who asks him to take part in a demonstration
on Friday, October 20, at the Department of Justice
where various groups of antiwar protesters intend to
relinquish their draft-cards to Attorney General Ramsey
Clark. Mailer arrives in Washington on October 19, for
previous to Goodman's phone call he had accepted an
invitation to speak at an antiwar rally at Washington's
old Ambassador Theater with three other literary men:
Robert Lowell, Paul Goodman, and Dwight Macdonald. Before the rally, he attends an insipid dinner
party hosted by academic liberals, at which he girds
himself with bourbon. Arriving late at the rally, he
hoists himself up on the stage, coaxes the program
coordinator, Ed de Grazia, aside, and, coffee mug
filled with bourbon, plays knavish Master of Ceremonies to the restless audience. To the displeasure
of his cospeakers, he holds forth in a profane harangue,
envisioning the rally as one great party. (In Mailer's
life and work, a party is an occasion for the moment
of truth, or potentially so. It is a witches' Sabbath

wherein masks are dissolved and the true contours of personality bared.) But this time Mailer effects an epiphany for no one. His rambling speech falls flat.

After some sleep at the Hay-Adams Hotel, Mailer appears at the Department of Justice Building where 994 draft-cards are collected at a draft resisters' ceremony. Aching with a hangover, he makes a modest speech before five hundred people. The next day, Saturday, the weather autumnally clear and bracing, he attends the pre-march rally at the Lincoln Memorial. Then, with a throng of forty to fifty thousand demonstrators, he marches across Arlington Memorial Bridge to the flat, vastly vapid grounds of the Pentagon. A rope sections off the crowd from the MPs. Mailer steps over it, slips past two MPs, sprints up to a group of U.S. Marshalls, and tells them he will go straight to the Pentagon if not arrested. They seize and book him; he spends the night in jail. An able lawyer gets him released on his own recognizance. On Sunday our cadgy picaro flies home to his family in New York.

The book's unity of time and its strict enclosure within the limits of a particular event and place give it a classical sharpness of design. There is a precision of vision here that we do not find in Mailer's previous two novels, *An American Dream* and *Why Are We in Vietnam?* Compelled into compliance with what he sees before him, he must now record reality rather than invent it. His previous novels shaped events; now events shape the book—events, moreover, that people know about and can therefore in some fashion relate to. Because *The Armies of the Night* does not require one to make the leap of imagination a fictional novel would demand, it proved to be for the American public Mailer's most readable book yet. Journalist Tom Wolfe comments on the winning qualities of the "new journalism."

[It] consumes devices that happen to have originated with
the novel and mixes them with every other device known to
prose. And all the while, quite beyond matters of technique,
it enjoys an advantage so obvious, so built-in, one almost
forgets what a power it has: the simple fact that the reader
knows *all this actually happened.* The disclaimers have
been erased. The screen is gone. The writer is one step
closer to the absolute involvement of the reader that
Henry James and James Joyce dreamed of and never
achieved.[1]

The Armies of the Night reclaimed for Mailer a popular and critical acclaim he had not known since the
publication of *The Naked and the Dead* twenty years
before.

What makes this book so extraordinarily engaging
is the characterization of the protagonist, Norman
Mailer. Usually he refers to himself simply as "Mailer"
or "he," but that he occasionally invokes other names
as well—the Ruminant, the Beast, the Existentialist,
the Historian, the Participant, the Novelist, the General, the Protagonist, Norman—attests to the mar-
velous diversity of his behavior, to the fact that all
along he is at will improvising identities the better
to accommodate himself to the multifariousness of
American society. An assumption guides him: in an
extremely pluralistic nation, the self, to operate effectively, must also be pluralistic.

Mailer's personality in this book can be accurately
described with a motley of adjectives: foolish, vain,
inspired, deluded, imaginative, energetic, generous,
quixotic. Interestingly, America itself can be accurately
described with the very same adjectives. This is a
recognition that Mailer expects us to arrive at, for he
imagines himself as a microcosm of the nation. He
believes that the conflicts raging within him are raging
within America—for example, the conflict between
domestic potential and world influence. As America

is torn between building a "great society" and diffusing
its energy to build a world economy based on capitalism, so is Mailer torn between writing a novel as
ambitious as *Moby-Dick* in order to satisfy his own
inner demands as an artist and churning out potboilers
for wide sales. That Mailer identifies his destiny with
America's reminds us of his Whitmanesque nature.
Like Walt Whitman he senses that his troubled soul
emanates from that larger troubled soul which is
America; that he sees himself as the embodiment of
his country also partly explains the robust openness
of his sensibility.

Not only Whitman's shade, but those of two other
writers—Ralph Waldo Emerson and Ernest Hemingway—reside in this book. When Emerson wrote "The
American Scholar" in 1837, he envisioned for America
a new breed of writer, one who, without sacrificing
the artistic integrity of his work, would be vigorously
involved in the important events of his own time and
free to comment upon them. He would be a man
whose writings would affect social and political life
in America. In *The Armies of the Night*, Mailer takes
it upon himself to give validity to Emerson's vision.
His march on the Pentagon, his subsequent arrest, his
writing of this book constitute his ardent attempt to
prove to the American public that the creative writer
can exercise a determining influence in the social-
political arena. Of course, as a child of New England
quietism, Emerson did not have militant activism in
mind for the American writer when he wrote "The
American Scholar," but, Mailer would argue, neither
did the relative cultural stability of the Jacksonian
era require it.

The other influence is that of Hemingway. As
Jake Barnes, the protagonist of *The Sun Also Rises*,
went to Pamplona to participate in the running of
the bulls, so does Mailer go to Washington to partici-

pate in the march on the Pentagon. Washington is
Mailer's Pamplona. It is a place seething with mass
excitement, a testing ground where man may seize
the chance to intrepidly pit his being against indomi-
table odds and, through the proper conjunction of
skill and luck, emerge not necessarily a winner but
more alive and aware than before. A *corrida de toros*
atmosphere pervades the antiwar march, however
much some of the demonstrators would be morally
embarrassed to admit it, having convinced themselves
that they are marching for non-selfish, humanistic
reasons; for, in other words, the people of Vietnam and
the withdrawal of American troops. But Mailer, never
one to let candor abate, realizes that most people have
come to Washington, as he has come, to confirm their
ability to be brave. He suggests that at forty-four he
has at least become wise enough to know that one
must gain honor for oneself before one can honestly
demand it be accorded to others.

Mailer knows, too, that as a writer he is up against
a social force that none of his literary forebears had to
contend with—a vast American populace that watches
TV, takes drugs, listens to records and tapes, goes to
the movies, and does not read literature. In recognition
of this hard fact, he feels compelled to make his
writing distinctly different from his forebears who also
wrote about the important political and social events
of their time. Mailer chooses to express himself in an
intricate and remarkably rich prose, a prose that carries with it a challenge. It is as though Mailer is saying
to the reader, "You're getting articulation now, dex-
terity of thought, the experience of which you must
reach for to feel. It will not come to you; you must
come to it. This is not TV." Mailer wants it under-
stood that the reality of events cannot be reduced to a
newscast or to newsprint. Only literature, he would
propose, can accurately render the multiplex nature

of experience. The continual modulations of mood, the convoluted and energetically reflective prose, that fill this book constitute Mailer's counterthrust against the mass media which, he believes, seduce the mind and make American society, particularly its adolescents, impatient with ideas, with situations of complexity, with the habit of reflection, the discerning of distinctions, the weight of nuance. The real excitement of *The Armies of the Night* for me derives from the drama of Mailer the writer in conflict with the American public rather than in the drama of Mailer the political malcontent in conflict with an oppressively technocratic state, symbolized by the Pentagon—a drama which has become by this time tiresomely repetitive after being treated previously in *Barbary Shore, Advertisements for Myself, The Presidential Papers, Cannibals and Christians,* and, most marvelously and incisively, in *Why Are We in Vietnam?*

Actually, the individual/state drama in this book turns out to be not so clear-cut a conflict as we might expect. While Mailer admires the demonstrators' pluck and wholeheartedly sympathizes with their moral stand against the state's authority, he makes it clear that both sides possess their share of lies, delusions, and dogmas. The young demonstrators, heads filled with ideational junk food and easy political formulas, are as doctrinaire, as incurious and inflexible, as the government they oppose. For this reason, and because the march, when it reaches the guarded Pentagon, becomes a sodden juggernaut with nowhere to go, Mailer decides to disengage himself from it and embark on a solo flight through the MP lines. At this point the sense of brotherly unity he felt with the marchers dissolves. One must admit it never did outweigh his vain sense of exclusive individuality.

Paradoxically, however, *The Armies of the Night* is as democratic a testimony as it is an egocentric one,

for in demonstrating with the famous—Robert Lowell,
Paul Goodman, Dwight Macdonald, Allen Ginsberg—
amid the horde, Mailer comes to recognize that the
famous are no more interesting or noble or significant
than anyone else. He finds the celebrity and the common man equally interesting. The famous because he
can explore beneath their official appearance, and
the common man because he can bestow on him the
status of celebrity. The book is rich with brilliantly
discerning portraits of the American character: the
West Virginia Marshall trying to do his decent best to
temper duty with conduct; the turnkey who, leading
Mailer down the prison hall so that he may telephone
his wife, exudes "narrowness, propriety, and goodwill,
and that infernal American innocence which could not
question one's leaders, for madness and boils of a
frustrated life resided beneath." Nor can we easily
forget Mailer's telling characterization of Lowell,
"virile and patrician and grim," who "gave off at times
the unwilling haunted saintliness of a man who was
repaying moral debts of ten generations of ancestors."
We are struck by the humanity of the book's personality sketches, by their breathing reality which
reminds us of how little difference in intensity there is
between the struggles of the famous and the struggles
of the individual at large.

Mailer is egocentric, yes, but we can never stop
there. Whatever we think of him, we do not think it
for long. The prismatic quality of his motivation is
what gives this book its radiant psychological reality.
We may decide, after the Ambassador Theater scene
for example, that he is the most abrasively attention-
getting and self-aggrandizing of men. Yet we cannot
help but admire a little later the unguarded honesty
of his self-analysis when, at the Department of Justice
Building, watching men his own age painfully relinquishing their draft-cards, he admits that for all his

humanist-liberal mouthings, he cannot muster the
courage or commitment to be one of them. These
men make him melancholic. They destroy his complacency. He stands uncomfortably in the cold, feeling
"himself becoming more and more of a modest man."

Truly Mailer is a self-preserving rogue, a character
of exorbitant disproportions, for always offsetting
every sacrificial act of civil disobedience is some ludi-
crous vanity that would make us wince were it not so
funny. He daringly instigates his arrest at the hands
of a U.S. Marshall, but a page later we learn that he
has engaged a filmmaker to follow him closely and
take movies of his arrest! Herded into an army truck
with the other prisoners, he finds it a "touch awkward"
climbing over the tailgate, "for he did not wish to
dirty his dark blue pinstripe suit." When he is finally
put behind bars, a single thought keeps recurring to
him. Can he be released in time to attend a Saturday-
night party in New York "which has every promise of
being wicked, tasty, and rich"? As one reviewer has
rightly observed:

Mailer not only feeds critics their ammunition on a tray,
he practically loads their guns and paints a bull's eye on
his heart. He is funnier and more devastating on the
subject of his vanity than anyone else will ever be. Can a
man be hung for ego madness who makes it as shrewd
an act as Jack Benny's stinginess?[2]

Mailer may not convince us as an earnest radical or
revolutionary hero or as a "Left-Conservative" (his
own term for himself) hero, but as a comic hero he is
a marvel.

That he can generate such self-satire is due largely
to his "command of a detachment, classic in severity
(for he was a novelist and so in need of studying
every last lineament of the fine, the noble, the frantic,
and the foolish in others and in himself)." And therein

lies the power of *The Armies of the Night*—in its
novelistic attributes, its stunning evocations of character and milieu and situation. When Mailer departs
from his novelistic rendering of material, the book
loses its thrust. The narrative-descriptive style, in
which explicit details triumphantly cohere with implicit moral moments, gives way to the oracular-
ruminative style which dotes on abstractions and cultural *cum* philosophical questions. The last paragraph
of the book is a case in point. Mailer imagines
"America, once a beauty of magnificence unparalleled,"
now horribly diseased because of her involvement in
the Southeast Asia war. He ponders her future:

She will probably give birth, and to what?—the most
fearsome totalitarianism the world has ever known? or can
she, poor giant, tormented lovely girl, deliver a babe of
a new world brave and tender, artful and wild? Rush to
the locks. Deliver us from our curse. For we must end on
the road to that mystery where courage, death, and the
dream of love give promise of sleep.

Such writing borders on cant and obscurity. How
unduly apocalyptic this passage seems now that American society has settled back into relative normality.

We may find Mailer as self-styled Jeremiah rather
tiresome. But when he goes about the business of
"studying" every "lineament" and exploring human
behavior with the old-fashioned tools of the novelist,
his writing wholly engages us. For sheer force of social
observation and astuteness of character delineation
The Armies of the Night is a considerable achievement. Most significantly, nowhere else in modern
American literature do we see a writer conceiving of
his life with such an abundance of drama, energy, and
wit. We have to go back to Benjamin Franklin, extraordinary as the association may seem, to find a
parallel.

Riding on a wave of critical applause for *The Armies of the Night*, Mailer went on again to cast himself as intimate witness to American history in the making. *Miami and the Siege of Chicago* is centered around the people and events of the Republican and Democratic National Conventions of August 1968. This time, however, Mailer the participant becomes comparatively self-effacing: he calls himself "the reporter," largely because he is under assignment with *Harper's* magazine to concentrate on personages and politics, not on himself. The book first appeared in the form of a 70,000-word article in *Harper's*. The introspective Mailer now defers to Mailer the journalist on the job.

The change in narrative role effects a change in narrative structure. *The Armies of the Night* seemed a crescendo; the action gradually mounted toward an explosive climax, the clash between demonstrators and soldiers. The book is one large wavelike movement. We remember *Miami and the Siege of Chicago*, on the other hand, as a slide show, a series of arresting images. To recount them is to convey the episodic nature of the book's plot: Miami Beach (center for the Republican convention), a synthetic city, atrocious in its commercial vulgarity, smothering one million years of jungle beneath its asphalt pavement; presidential candidate Nelson Rockefeller ever ready to play down his patrician bearing with an affable grin; the Grand Gala at the Fontainebleau Hotel where the nation's prosperous WASPs gather together and bathe themselves in the hope that a Republican president may lead them back to "their lost America"; Richard Nixon, awkwardly cheerful with close to six hundred delegates committed to him, responding to the press with scrupulously banal pronouncements designed to alienate no one; the Reverend Ralph D. Abernathy (leader of the Poor People's March after the assassina-

tion of Martin Luther King), a harried man of precarious dignity, cast into a position of immense
responsibility too early; presidential contender Ronald
Reagan, all poise and style, tempering his Hollywood
image with the sober-mindedness of a banker; Nixon's
acceptance speech, filled with appeasements for left,
center, and right, which leaves Mailer not knowing
whether to like or to detest him for his implacable
shrewdness.

When Mailer shifts focus to Chicago (seat of the
Democratic convention), his slide show glows with
life. As good as the writing is in Part One, "Nixon in
Miami," in Part Two, "The Siege of Chicago," it is
better. Mailer describes Chicago—the processes of
animal slaughter in its stockyards, its architecture, the
strengths of its ethnic neighborhoods—with such
articulate sensuousness and sharp intensity of detail
that it remains one of the most powerful portraits of
that city ever written. To get from Chicago to a
description of the 5000 supporters of presidential candidate Eugene McCarthy, Mailer invokes a Rabelaisian
image for transition: if one could imagine Chicago as
a human face, a "broad fleshy nose" would be its most
prominent feature, a nose "open wide to stench, stink,
power, a pretty day, a well-stacked broad, and the
beauties of a dirty buck." In contrast, the supporters
of Eugene McCarthy have "thin nostrils," which suggest to Mailer that like their candidate they are
parsimonious in distributing sympathy to either the
left or the right of the traditional political spectrum.
McCarthy, coolly immured in elegant calm, makes his
points with deft reticence, choosing to believe, Mailer
implies, that he is above politics. But later in the book
when Mailer unexpectedly meets him in a restaurant,
the senator's face expresses an arch toughness. He
could very well have been an uncorruptible, iron-
willed police commissioner.

Mailer sees presidential contender Hubert Humphrey as McCarthy's opposite, characterizing the long-time senator from Minnesota, and now Vice-President to Lyndon Johnson, as a man immersed in the stews of political give and take. When Humphrey wins the Democratic nomination, Mailer takes note of his acceptance speech and sarcastically wonders at the relevance of its patriotic fervor in view of the fact that outside the convention hall Chicago is in the throes of a massive riot. Antiwar people—mostly hippies and Yippies (Youth International Party)— driven by helmeted police from their meeting place in Lincoln Park, roam the streets in marauding bands. Mayor Richard Daley calls in the National Guard. On Michigan Avenue outside the Conrad Hilton, the police run amok, attacking not only demonstrators but delegates and innocent bystanders as well. From their rooms in the Hilton, candidates and delegates watch the beatings below in utter dismay.

When the convention ends, the smoke clears; and Mailer, thoroughly exhausted after unsuccessfully trying to lead two hundred delegates in an antiwar march from Grant Park to the convention hall, meets with drinking friends to soothe away the psychic abrasions of four calamitous days. He ends his book with a small rumination on Mayor Daley. The mayor is a "bullfrog" of a man, staunch and severe, but in his soft jowls one can envisage the gradual weakening of authoritarian force in America. "Put your fingers in V for victory and give a wink," Mailer tells the reader, imagining himself as one comrade talking to another. "We may yet win, the others are so stupid. Heaven help us when we do."

To drive to the inner truth of these conventions, Mailer employs a veritable arsenal of expository modes—the political scientist's, the hard boiled detective's, the prophet's, the metaphysician's, the sociolo-

gist's, the psychologist's—and galvanizes them with
the imagination of a poet. His metaphors always reach
beyond the subject they attend to—whether it be a
place, an individual, an event—to show that subject in
its widest, most revealing, cultural significance. Here,
for example, is a description of the Miami Beach
skyline:

For ten miles, from the Diplomat to the DiLido, . . . all the
white refrigerators six and eight and twelve stories high,
shaped like sugar cubes and ice-cube trays on edge, like
mosques and palaces, shaped like matched white luggage
and portable radios, stereos, plastic compacts and plastic
rings. Moorish castles shaped like waffle irons, shaped like
the baffle plates on white plastic electric heaters, and
cylinders like Waring blenders, buildings looking like giant
op art and pop art paintings, and sweet wedding cakes,
cottons of kitsch and piles of dirty cotton stucco . . .

We can see from this passage how Mailer can elicit
from a given stimulus an aggregate richness of cultural
meaning that vies with the cinematic and televised
image. He is always endeavoring to beat the media
at their own game, and usually does so. For compared
to anything the media can produce, how very much
more interesting and provocative, it seems to me, is
Mailer's mind, which it would not be implausible to
characterize as a vast spiderweb of sensitive threads
catching every air-borne particle of experience and
transforming it to revelation.

    At the Republican convention, however, revela-
tion does not come easy to Mailer. In fact, its dullness
exasperates him and he soon realizes that to find its
excitement, if excitement it has, he must dig beneath
surfaces. And so he does. He develops a burrowing
eye. All externals—a candidate's face, his walk, the
tenor of his voice—he learns to read as indexes to the
personal anxieties that seethe beneath. He digs under
the lusterless rhetoric of the speeches to discover the

raw egotism that drives each candidate on. As a politician himself—he tells us in *Advertisements for Myself* that he has "been running for President . . . in
the privacy" of his "own mind" (and in 1969 he runs
for mayor of New York)—he has a shrewd, intimate
understanding of political life. He knows that the
American politician in high office, however smooth
his outward manner may appear, paces a catwalk
between honor and shame; that each presidential contender is a larger-than-life projection of the hopes and
banalities, the energies and obstinacies, the humilities
and complacencies, the kindnesses and cupidities of
the nation itself.

Mailer can closely observe the people and personages who comprise the conventions, largely because
he is so seldom recognized as Norman Mailer, celebrated author. This fact, interestingly, enhances rather
than retards his reportorial skills. At the Republican
Grand Gala, for example, hardly anyone knows or
probably cares who he is. Inundated by WASP wealth
and power, this big-time New Yorker is compelled
into a hard reassessment of his own measure. He drifts
anonymously through the ballroom. Yet his incon-
spicuousness allows him to study freely the characters
of the guests. The result is a remarkably perceptive
chapter on "the muted tragedy of the WASP" in
America:

In their immaculate cleanliness, in the somewhat antiseptic
odors of their astringent toilet water and perfume, in the
abnegation of their walks, in the heavy sturdy moves so
many demonstrated of bodies in life's harness . . . they
were not on earth to enjoy or even perhaps to love so very
much, they were here to serve, and serve they had in
public functions and public charities (while recipients of
their charity might vomit in rage and laugh in scorn),
served on opera committees, and served in long hours of
duty at the piano, served as the sentinel in concert halls

and pews on the aisle in church, at the desk in schools,
had served for culture, had served for finance, served for
salvation, served for America—and so much of America
did not wish them to serve any longer, and so many of
them doubted themselves, doubted that the force of their
faith could illumine their path in these new modern
horror-head times.

Yet whatever the cultural or political background
of the delegates at these conventions, Mailer believes
that one principle propels them all: "Politics is
property." To understand this principle (first pro-
pounded by Murray Kempton, Democratic delegate
from New York) is to understand how delegates
jockey for position. Their vote is their property. They
will relinquish it or compromise it only for self-gain.
They hold on to it as dearly as a man holds on to his
house and will consider giving it up only for bigger
property, that is, for more power. A candidate's stand
on a given issue is also property. He will subdivide
his property when he thinks there is strength in numbers. Only then will he admit to his agreement with
others on a particular issue. He will lease his property
if his stand on an issue seems to be losing popularity,
only to make a trade for it later on when the issue
regains respect. He stakes out his property with great
care and always tries to be first at the starting gate
for a land grab. "End the war in Vietnam," "Law and
order now," are two properties that every political
master and piker bought up as soon as they came on
the market. Mailer gives us the "politics is property"
metaphor to play with, to expand upon at will, and to
imagine a political equivalent to equity, mortgages,
taxes. It is an enlightening and useful metaphor. It
is what helps to make *Miami and the Siege of Chicago*
the canniest book on American politics ever written
by a novelist.

Mailer's next book again combines a "good story"

—a story of immediate topical value—with philosophical depth and perspective. *Of a Fire on the Moon*
is concerned with the voyage of the Apollo 11 astronauts (Neil Armstrong, Buzz Aldrin, and Mike Col-
lins) from the earth to the moon and back in the
summer of 1970. It is divided into three parts:
"Aquarius," "Apollo," and "The Age of Aquarius."
Part II, the longest and least engaging section, deals
far more with the technical procedures of the space
flight than with its meaning. It is a veritable manual
of astronautical operations that baffle and amaze the
reader who is not a space engineer. Finding himself
inside the belly of that huge technocracy called NASA
(National Aeronautics and Space Administration),
Mailer transforms his perspective accordingly and
becomes the technocrat to beat all technocrats, exhaustively detailing the intricate mechanical grandeur
of the Apollo-Saturn rocket. He does so, however, in
the service of art, not in the service of science. I am
an epical poet, he seems to be saying, and therefore
take all human experience as my province. No disci-
pline is foreign to me. Within me lie the capabilities
of all men and I can successfully try my hand at whatever their trade may be. I can be an engineer and a
poet and everything in between. With such Whitmanesque assumptions Mailer forges out Part II, and
by so doing claims for the artist a versatility of mind
that is not possible, he suggests, for the expert, who
must necessarily be confined within the boundaries
of his own small plot of knowledge.

Parts I and III, which concentrate on the meaning
of the Apollo 11 flight, are by far the most memorable
sections of the book. Abandoning "the reporter" persona of *Miami and the Siege of Chicago,* Mailer
assumes a new persona, "Aquarius," the sign of the
truth-seeker. The chief characteristic of the Aquarius
type is breadth of vision. Yet, despite the vibrancy of

Mailer's descriptions, the impression one gets is of a
vision sought rather than found. Apollo 11's flight, as
momentous as Mailer admits it is, does not finally
bring him any closer, as he so ardently hoped it would,
to a clarifying conception of man's role in the universe.
Is the Apollo-Saturn rocket an instrument of the Devil?
Or is it a symbol of the will of God, a God who has
enjoined man to help Him effect a fuller actualization
of His power in the universe? These questions rever-
berate throughout the book and comprise its basic
philosophical tension. But they are questions Mailer
finds himself unable to answer; and he urgently needs
to, for as a Manichean he believes that all energy
emanates from either of two contending principles—
the power of darkness or the power of light.

    Mailer is ambivalent toward the moon flight. His
grandiloquent pronouncements about how Faustian,
ominous, affirmative and ennobling it is leave us feeling
ambivalent toward it too. The book ends inconclusively
with Aquarius in the Manned Spacecraft Center at
Houston sniffing away at a small moon rock hermeti-
cally sealed within two layers of glass. A nebulously
intuitive ending, it leaves us unsatisfied. The moon
rock smells to him like the "cleanest hay" and like the
"subtle lift of love which comes from the cradle of
the new born." We want something at once more
imaginative and more palpable than this. We would
like to depend on more than Mailer's nose to understand the significance of the greatest odyssey man has
ever undertaken.

    The curious irony of this book is that the essential
mystery of the Apollo 11 mission is the astronauts,
not the moon. They constitute the paradox at the heart
of the Apollo 11 project. Their total lack of magic
makes them for Mailer as enigmatic as anything that
lies beyond the stars. They are pioneers, yet speak a
language so stale and cliché-ridden and infused with

"computerese" that we are led to wonder just what powers of inventiveness they really do possess. They remind Mailer of the argonauts, if he could forget that they behave like corporation executives. If they are "saints," they are "robots" as well because they have become the living tools of NASA. For a successful space flight, that is as it should be. Only insofar as man approximates an automaton can he successfully reach the moon. But Mailer, arch romantic that he is, refuses to admit to such a proposition. To do so would be, he feels, to acknowledge the moon landing as a "giant step" *backward* "for all mankind."

Mailer cannot see in the astronauts' struggle the magnitude he wants to see, for they are unalienated. An unalienated man is alien to Norman Mailer. The astronauts are not fighting against oppression. They are not examples of beleaguered individuality. They are not rebellious. This is all to say that by the terms of Mailer's vision of life they do not embody the highest order of bravery and dignity. The hero for Mailer is a man who maintains an adversative relation to the world. From *The Naked and the Dead* on, living creatively has meant living *against* something as much as it has meant living *for* something. W. H. Auden's injunction—"We must love one another or die"—would be more agreeable to Mailer if it were "We must fight one another or die." To oppose is to grow. If malevolence did not exist, Mailer would be impelled to invent it. That the astronauts have readily conformed their lives to the powers that be, namely to the corporate-industrial-military matrix that constitutes for Mailer the American state, makes it impossible for him to view them as heroes.

Armstrong's fathomless blandness, his impeccability of manner and mood, disconcert Mailer and lead him to suggest that to be so neatly and totally programmed is not to be your own man. He acknowledges

the apocalyptic magnificence of Armstrong's deed, but
cannot render Armstrong's valor as brilliantly as he
can his unparalleled banality. "The American cool was
becoming a narcotic. The horror of the Twentieth
Century was the size of each new event, and the
paucity of its reverberation."

A cultural gap separates Mailer from the astronauts. He is a New York Jew. They are small-town
WASPs. He shares in the heritage of Marx and Freud.
They are heirs of capitalism and science. And so he
invites us to conclude that the moon mission may
very well be a logical extension of the historic WASP
pattern of dominance—first the red man, then the
black man, then the yellow man, now the extrater-
restrial realm. Whether we concur with this or not,
we cannot help agreeing with Mailer that what the
moon mission means to the American people is an
attestation of man's control over nature, not a redis-
covery of his mysterious partnership with it.

In all Mailer's reservations about the mission,
however, we hear the rumblings of his own ambitious
ego. A manned flight to the moon, he insists, can
bring us to a clarifying conception of man's role in the
universe only if it is an experience lived through by
an individual of the imagination—by, in short, the
artist. In this suggestion lies the problem of the book
because Mailer cannot make poetry or a drama of
dread out of "technologese" (for example, man's first
step on the moon is termed an EVA, Extravehicular
Activity) and so one is put in closer touch with pro-
cedure than with power. The personnel at NASA are
too insulated, too conditioned, ever to convince our
imaginations of the majesty of their endeavor. Later
flights, Mailer hopes, will be freer and show a wider
variety of human response and therefore be at last an
invitation to the perceptual powers of the poet.
". . . yes, we might have to go out into space until

the mystery of new discovery would force us to regard the world once again as poets, behold it as savages who knew that if the universe was a lock, its key was metaphor rather than measure." Man monitored by computers, enveloped by vinyl, smog, and plastic, deluded by the media, anesthetized by air-conditioning and pills, will, Mailer believes, expire on the dissection table of technology unless the poet, through the inventive powers of language, inspires him to think, to wonder, to imagine, and to dream.

9

○○○○○○○○○○○○○○○○○○○○○○○○○○○○○○○○○○○○○○○

Awesome Women:
The Prisoner of Sex and *Marilyn*

In the opening pages of *The Prisoner of Sex*, Mailer tells us that in the late spring of 1970 he went on a vacation to Maine with five of his six children. The unending tasks of housework consume his time, and on top of it all he must look after his children. He finds himself pitched into the mundane, a realm more foreign to his life than anything else, and begins to understand the dismal drudgery a housewife daily contends with. Greasy pots and ironing may very well be, he imagines, the plank and beam of female thralldom.

Unable to withstand for long the chores of running a home, Mailer calls for aid. His sister assists for two weeks, then he invites his mistress up and hires a cleaning woman. Family outings, good food, the blue waterways of Somes Sound promise a restful summer. Mailer the proud paterfamilias is a warmly engaging self-portrait of which we get merely a glimpse. Familial feelings and the healing qualities of nature are subjects one is unused to in his writing. He handles them well.

While Mailer was packing picnic lunches for seaside rambles, leading exponents of the new feminism, "a squadron of enraged Amazons, an honor guard of revolutionary vaginas," launched an attack on him in the New York press. Months before he had read Mary Ellmann's *Thinking about Women* (1968) and felt its sardonic barbs, but Kate Millett's *Sexual*

Politics (1970) and a cover story on her in *Time* magazine ignite him. Millett declares him to be the very embodiment of what is most repugnant to the new feminism: male dominance and sexual exploitation. The movement has gained too much momentum for a defense, Mailer thinks. So he brings out instead all his verbal artillery—polemic, poetry, burlesque, pun, invective—and launches an unstoppered counterattack. The result is *The Prisoner of Sex*.

To do battle with the new feminists, Mailer assumes four personas: "The Prizewinner" (Part I), "The Acolyte" (Part II), "The Advocate" (Part III), and "The Prisoner" (Part IV).

The Prizewinner is Norman Mailer, illustrious, best-selling author and contender for the Nobel Prize. But, as always, beneath his self-touting he lodges a fuse of self-irony: if he has been triumphant in his work, he wants us to know that he has been a loser at love. In fact, the new feminists attack him when he is down; one purpose of his summer in Maine is to lick the wounds inflicted from a fourth failed marriage. Paradoxically, though, their attack comes at just the right time. It is necessary now, Mailer thinks, to reexplore his relationship with women by examining the nature of his love for them and to once and for all set forth in writing his own ideas about the sex game and his own sexuality. *The Prisoner of Sex*, then, is an act of self-clarification. The further Mailer ponders the new feminism the more he comes to realize that it is a subject unexpectedly rich in possibilities. After all,

the themes of his life had gathered here. Revolution, tradition, sex and the homosexual, the orgasm, the family, the child and the political shape of the future, technology and human conception, waste and abortion, the ethics of the critic and the male mystique, black rights and new thoughts on women's rights.

Recognizing that the new feminism is a pervasive subculture about which he knows too little, Mailer casts himself in the role of "Acolyte" and sets out to read the literature of the movement. He is impressed. The prose vibrates with muscle and authority. It is charged with a gusto and a candor he had all too presumptuously supposed to be qualities of male writers alone.

But of the ideas that are the propulsive force behind this new prose, Mailer can accept only two: women are economically exploited in the job market and the home; only revolution will erase the inequalities from which they—and men too—suffer. Yet Mailer does not say how revolution can be successfully effected. Like many a veteran leftist, he has an approach-avoidance reaction to revolution. It is "either the most beautiful or diabolical of ideas."

Economic and social rights, Mailer makes clear, are one thing; physiological rights are another. The freedom that Kate Millett envisions for women once technology delivers them from the bondage of the womb, Mailer can only perceive as a deeper bondage for the whole human race. Semen banks, genetic engineering, artificial wombs, human birth by parthenogenesis—all such schemes for a scientifically immaculate conception he regards as totalitarian stratagems leading to world-wide homogeneity. To liberate woman from childbearing is "a way of guaranteeing that the end game of the absurd is coitus-free conception monitored by the state." In Mailer's archromantic view, to tamper with natural biological conception and gestation is to cripple human evolution. The womb, he believes, is the house of propitious conjunction where Creation tries to harmonize its polarities, symbolized by the sperm and the egg, in order to bring itself further toward perfection by a process "deeper than reason."

Accusing Mailer of undue mythicizing, of blurring the point, the new feminists say that unwanted conception thrusts woman into obligation and guilt: obligation to child and husband; guilt born of recrimination against them for placing her in servitude. Confronted with what he can only interpret as a perversely idolatrous regard for technology, Mailer serves up his customary blend of sulfur and wit. If woman's fealty is to a mini vacuum cleaner, the tubular curette, "TECHNOLOGY SUCKS would appear on no placards carried by woman."

On the question of the sex act itself, Mailer, long-time mystagogue of orgasmic ecstasy, scorns those feminists who applaud Doctors Masters and Johnson, the experimental sexologists who rescued their patients from frigidity and impotence by encouraging them, in comfortable laboratory conditions, to use those stimulative techniques most conducive to orgasmic gratification. Plastic dildoes, people in laboratories making love with wires attached to them, clitoral versus vaginal orgasm—all this, complains Mailer, is so clinical, so vapid, so very much beside the point. Sexuality is not genitality. Rather, he insists, it has to do—and he quotes William Blake—with "comminglings from the Head to the Feet." Doctors Masters and Johnson are able to calibrate the periodicity and count of orgasms on electronic machines, but Mailer intends us to believe that neither they nor their machines can calibrate human experience, the sensibility in orgasm. A middle-aged matron, successful laboratory subject, may say in flushed delirium, "I came fifty times." But, Mailer implies, only a man of imagination, a novelist, can decipher the message of her orgasm, can tell the metaphysical steeps and gulfs she has vaulted and plumbed: "contemplate comings as far away as the aria and the hunt and the devil's own ice of a dive, orgasms like the collision of a truck, or coming soft as snow, or slipping in with the sweaty heat of a slide down slippery slopes."

But no, says Millett in *Sexual Politics*. The male novelist, however much he may claim to know the female sensibility, has miserably failed to authentically render it. As two cases in point, she pillories Henry Miller and D. H. Lawrence. At this juncture Mailer exchanges his "Acolyte" role for one of "Advocate" and argues in support of his brother artists. For Millett, Miller is America's vile pasha of depersonalized sex. She cites passages from his early novels, *Tropic of Cancer* (1934) and *Tropic of Capricorn* (1939), in which, she contends, men use women as mere carnal fodder. But Mailer accuses Millett of hypocrisy here: though she deplores Miller's use of women as sexual provender, she staunchly supports the idea that the female may use the male for no more than her own sexual gratification. Mailer is at his comic and mischievous best defending his crony in eroticism and lampooning Millett for what he deems her dogged, tractarian approach, her insensitivity to Miller's humor and metaphoric power—in short, her lack of literary-critical skill. And she lacks literary-historical knowledge too, Mailer suggests, for she has not recognized the fact that Henry Miller is a pioneer. He introduced sexual intercourse as a subject proper for fiction of artistic seriousness and thereby enriched and broadened the novel. Before Miller no noted American novelist had ever presumed that a life devoted to sexual gratification could provide material for art. Mailer believes that lust is a subject the understanding of which goes a long way in clarifying what it is to be human and alive. And who can say, he asks, that it is not the threshold to love?

If Mailer plays literary critic in appraising Miller, with D. H. Lawrence he plays psychoanalyst. The man

Millett accuses of denying the individuality of the
female personality and proclaiming the glory of sexual
tyranny over women is the man Mailer sees as so
outrageously possessed by his mother's smothering
love that only by dominating woman in the sex act
could he rouse his virility to the "height from which
it might seek transcendence." Sexual transcendence
was the very bread of Lawrence's life. It was, according to Mailer, "the ecstasy where he could lose his ego
for a moment, his sense of self and his will . . ." Mailer
refutes Millett's charge that the sexual act in
Lawrence's *oeuvre* is a matter of male will and female
submission. *Both* sexes must deliver themselves, in
Lawrence's words, "over to the unknown" and submit
to it. Thus man and woman lay themselves open to
seizure by a mystical power greater than themselves;
to the Creator, Mailer prefers to think.

Mailer suspects Millett of not having much use
for God or any other mystery. Assured that the "sexes
are alike in everything save reproductive systems,"
she proposes that aggressiveness and passivity, qualities traditionally ascribed to male and female respectively, be eradicated by social engineering and that
socially desirable traits be "disseminated." "The re-
mark," says Mailer, "opened the door to eugenics, and
beyond was the stuff of experimental control in the
extra-uterine womb . . ." Moreover, when contraception
removes from the sex act the intimate awe of conceiving life, heterosexual intercourse will become, he
admonishes, like homosexual intercourse, "a clearing
house for power, a market for psychic power in which
the stronger will use the weaker." Heterosexual intercourse, as the new feminists envisage it, sounds, he
says, like the homosexual coupling that Jean Genet
describes in his novel on prison life, *Our Lady of the
Flowers.*

Mailer graces the womb, envisioning it as woman's

alliance with eternity, her inner cosmos. And man the striver must buy into that cosmos because he is isolated from it. Having no womb, man is separated from nature, heroically alone. Sexual intercourse is an apocalyptically grave engagement in which the sperm, writhing "limb of the soul seeking to be born," takes a leap toward "every call of the woman for what was magnificent or large as her idea of future life." Claiming percipience for the ovum, Mailer ecstatically visualizes it as an expectant priestess choosing to receive only the most valiant of wriggling voyagers that enter through her door.

Following what he calls "metaphysical drift," Mailer makes other astounding claims: the quality of copulation can determine the quality of offspring; women in the sex act possess a subconscious power to accept or reject fertilization. He sounds more convinced than convincing when the poet in him overwhelms the thinker. His arguments tend to be facile. And one even wonders how far we can separate him from the totalitarian motives he accuses sexual politician Millett of. When he writes in *The Armies of the Night* that "the majority of demonstrators, if one counted the women, had never marched in ranks before," he is unintentionally revealing chauvinism in an offhand phrase. Why shouldn't one count the women?

It is as a poet rather than as a polemicist that Mailer becomes most vulnerable. The more poetically he treats sexuality the more meaning he attaches to it, until in Part IV he becomes "The Prisoner": "No thought was so painful as the idea that sex had meaning: for give meaning to sex and one was the prisoner of sex—the more meaning one gave it, the more it assumed, until every failure and misery, every evil of your life, spoke their lines in its light, and every fear of mediocre death."

But also, for Mailer, every honor, every hope and
virtue, makes itself manifest in sex. He believes in this
book, as he always has, that to a great extent what
you are is how you copulate, that the sex act is the
barometer of personality. We might interpret *The
Prisoner of Sex*, then, as Mailer's wily toast to the new
feminists for making possible an opportunity to
ruminate, by way of an attack on them, on the deepest
reaches of his self.

A question remains. Do Mailer's ideas about
women in this book correspond to implicit ideas
articulated in his novels or has Mailer the middle-aged
man changed his views? Actually, his views have not
altered. He still sees women as adversaries, as biological shamans, as beings capable of bequeathing to
man godlike powers and of utterly mortifying him.
But Mailer's work depends on them, and he knows it.
Many of his books could hardly have been written had
he not been loving or hating a woman at the time of
writing.

Interestingly, when *The Prisoner of Sex* came out
most feminists received it with equanimity, though
Brigid Brophy criticized both Mailer and Millett for
doing an injustice to the sexes and called their inflated
infighting "a revival of the traditional slapstick of sex
hostility" that, "dehumanizing us all," further retards
what we need most, "a vast movement of Human
Lib."[1] And Joyce Carol Oates charged Mailer with
"dreamy illogic." To deny woman "choice in the
matter of reproduction, as we would never do in the
matter of, say, ordinary medicine or dentistry, seems
an empty sentimentality."[2]

Issues aside, however, what seems most unfortu-
nate about this book is its style. Although *The Prisoner
of Sex* comprises Mailer's most energetic expository
prose since "The White Negro" fourteen years earlier,
too often he and the reader lose the flow of argument

in a rip tide of endless sentences swirling with the debris of subpoints and elaborate qualifiers. The reader needs a blue pencil.

Nonetheless, when Mailer is propelling home a point with hard imagery, as he does in his discussion of Miller and Lawrence and in his description of the subterranean drama of the sperm and the ovum, his language sharpens. It becomes trenchant and self-delighting. And always there is malice toward none. He cajoles, grins, struts, goads, mocks, beguiles, and in the end is willing to concede to the new feminists the justice of their claim to equal social, political, and economic rights. Because of the inestimable value of these rights to himself, he can empathize with the feminists' demand for them.

So let woman be what she would, and what she could. Let her cohabit on elephants if she had to, and . . . with Borzoi hounds . . . yes, give her freedom and let her burn it, or blow it, or build it to triumph or collapse. Let her conceive her children, and kill them in the womb if she thought they did not have it, let her travel to the moon, write the great American novel, and allow her husband to send her off to work with her lunch pail and a cigar.

He is willing to concede woman everything except relinquishment of the womb. That he cannot abide. Ending the embryo or relegating a fertilized egg to the petri dish of extra-uterine conception is for him god-lessness. If every conception is an annunciation or potentially so, "who," he asks, "was there to know that God was not the greatest lover of them all?" Let not technology exclude Him.

A year after *The Prisoner of Sex* was published Mailer again braced himself to take the plunge into the female psyche. He was offered a large sum of money to write a preface to accompany a photographic retrospect of Marilyn Monroe. Long fascinated with persons who, like himself, have been intimate with the

prizes and perils of playing to a national audience, he
could not resist expanding his 25,000-word preface to
a 93,000-word "novel biography." After all, he realized,
here was a chance to explore in writing a spiritual twin.

Marilyn is a rapidly paced book exhibiting a
shrewd, cosmopolitan understanding of American life.
Mailer delineates the attitudes and posings of each
cultural arena Monroe passed through during her
fated career: the pious home life of Wayne and Ida
Bolender, her small-town foster parents; the cold,
grasping ambition of studio contract players at
Twentieth Century-Fox; the synthetic world of international stardom; the exclusive societies of sportsmen
(Joe DiMaggio, her second husband) and *litterateurs*
(Arthur Miller, her third husband); the proud high-
mindedness of New York theatrical circles.

Mailer never met Monroe, so for factual informa-
tion he heavily relies, by his own admission, on two
previous biographies: *Marilyn Monroe* by Maurice
Zolotow and *Norma Jean* by Fred Guiles. Using as a
basis the history of Monroe that Zolotow and Guiles
provide, he develops his favorite theories of magic and
dread to move more deeply than they into the
mysteries that surrounded her. For example, when
Natasha Lytess, Monroe's solicitously devoted drama
coach, said that her pupil needed her the way " 'a
dead man needs a coffin,' " Mailer takes the statement
to mean that the deepest motivations of Monroe's
acting were inseparable from "magic incantation, spell,
and necrophilia." A page later he writes that she
infused her artistry with "the transmutations of a
sorceress" while studying at Lee Strasberg's Actor's
Studio in New York, which he compares to "a cavern
where mysteries of acting are evoked in soul-shifting
states of ceremony." Her life is surrounded with
"omens." Her pregnant mother did not abort her
(Marilyn was conceived out of wedlock) because an

"inner imperative may have told her this child was too special to abort." And her suicide, says Mailer, may have been induced by singing voices from eternity telling her to take a "leap to leave the pain of one . . . soul for the hope of life in another."

When Mailer is not sheathing Monroe in the supernatural, he is showing us what a master of paradox she was. There is no trait we can ascribe to her, he contends, without its opposite also being true.

Since she was also a movie star of the most stubborn secretiveness and flamboyant candor, most conflicting arrogance and on-rushing inferiority; great populist of philosophers—she loved the working man—and most tyrannical of mates, a queen of a castrator who was ready to weep for a dying minnow; a lover of books who did not read, and a proud, inviolate artist who could haunch over to publicity when the heat was upon her faster than a whore could lust over a hot buck; a female spurt of wit and sensitive energy who could hang like a sloth for days in a muddy-mooded coma; a child-girl, yet an actress to loose a riot by dropping her glove at a premiere; a fountain of charm and a dreary bore; an ambulating cyclone of beauty when dressed to show, a dank hunched-up drab at her worst—with a bad smell!—a giant and an emotional pygmy; a lover of life and a cowardly hyena of death who drenched herself in chemical stupors; a sexual oven whose fire may rarely have been lit—she would go to bed with her brassiere on—she was certainly more and less the silver witch of us all.

Monroe was a virtuoso of contraries. And her photographs seem to bear this out. She does not look the same in any two. Mailer invites us to conclude that she is beguilingly undefinable. Most of the facts about her are not really facts at all, he says, but "factoids," that is, exaggerations, distortions, and conjectures created by gossip-mongers and released to the media. Monroe herself was a contributor. She had been "publishing her fables for years."

Mailer's contention is that if the real Monroe is to be discovered, a novelist must do it. To conceive of her novelistically, his premise goes, is to come closer than any purely biographical reportage can to the truth of what her "unspoken impulses" were. "Exceptional people have a way of living with opposites in themselves" that puts them beyond the pale of logical inquiry and renders traditional "biographical tools" insufficient. This is a large surmise on Mailer's part, one that in its inference does not acknowledge many a praiseworthy biography on many an exceptional person. However, even if we do grant Mailer his purpose in *Marilyn*—to set an artist to catch an artist and write a novel-biography—we have to question whether he has really evoked for us the originality of her character. As Mailer treats her, she seems less a character in her own unique right than a composite portrait of his former female creations. She is blowzy and defiant, like Guinivere McLeod in *Barbary Shore*. Like Elena Esposito in *The Deer Park*, she panics at the thought of her own inadequacies. She is wanton yet angel-pure like Cherry Melanie in *An American Dream*. A dazzle of schizophrenic complexity, she resembles Hallie Jethro in *Why Are We in Vietnam?* More than once Mailer calls Monroe a ghost, for the memory of her beauty, her triumph, her tragedy continued to haunt the American mind eleven years after her death. Inhabited by Mailer's former female characters, she is a ghost inhabited by ghosts, and so our difficulty in attaining some kind of vision of the person she really was is compounded.

Still there are passages in which Mailer allows authenticated biographical material to firmly prescribe his themes. Such passages are the only effective parts of the book. Dramatically insightful is his understanding of Monroe's two marriages and the cultural milieu in which they effervesced and foundered. He astutely describes Joe DiMaggio and his sports-loving cronies as possessive of their women, hostilely suspicious of art and acting. To insure conjugal success, Monroe transforms herself into "the queen of the working class." She becomes DiMaggio's trophy, and he is happy. Later, she can no longer distinguish his love from his shackling chauvinism and breaks away from him to immerse herself more than ever in her career. For Arthur Miller, she becomes "a Jewish princess." She converts to Judaism, keeps a kosher home, and adoringly basks in the glows of his kindly intellectual wisdom. But their marriage is destined for dissolution. They have false expectations of each other. She is overly dependent and keeps him from his work, and he never, to her satisfaction, "open[s] the life of the mind to her." They are sexually incompatible. She has an affair with Yves Montand.

When Mailer responsibly welds his literary talents to the role of cultural critic he is a delight to read. Novelistic and biographical impulse perfectly merge, neither weakening the other. But the further he diverges from the facts the more he lapses into turgidity. One shudders for his writing when it veers off the straight road of concrete description onto the soft shoulders of abstraction. For example, what sense can we grasp from his explanation of how Ingmar Bergman puts his personal imprint on film? ". . . All the hoarded haunted sorrows of Scandinavia drift in to imbibe the vampires of his psyche—he is like a spirit vapor risen out of the sinister character of film itself." Such writing generates more heat than light. Another example: Monroe proves herself a "great comedian" in *Gentlemen Prefer Blondes*, "which is to say she bears an exquisitely light relation to the dramatic thunders of triumph, woe, greed, and calculation." Hardly a clarifying definition of a great come-

dian. Long priding himself on being one of the fastest
writers alive—he has entitled one piece "Ten Thousand Words a Minute" (*The Presidential Papers*)—
Mailer wrote *Marilyn* in two months in order to get it
published for the summer-fall book season. It seems
that power and precision of language have been sacri-
ficed to the requirements of time.

And it is a pity, for the thesis of *Marilyn* is
profound. Monroe's selfhood, the identity she des-
perately groped for all her life, was a mirage. Not
able to find it by her own efforts, she sought out other
people—her husbands, agents, directors—to help her
find it. Unsatisfied with the results of the impossible
task she set them, she sought solace in pills. Her
search for an identity beneath or beyond her multiple
roles was necessarily futile because, Mailer believes,
identity exists *within* roles. Our manner of appearing
is our manner of being. The mask is the face. Role *is*
identity, a fulfilling identity if one's role is self-created,
not imposed from without by a studio, an audience,
or a husband. Here, then, we have a clue to Mailer's
own behavior. His identity is self-created and de-
liberately prismatic. He is "the reporter" in *Miami
and the Siege of Chicago*. In *The Armies of the Night*
he is master of ceremonies, general, actor, director,
ambassador, banker, historian, and novelist. Since
Advertisements for Myself the assumption of Mailer's
books has been that if identity is diversified, it is more
difficult for internal and external suppressors—the
superego and the state—to retard individual growth.
Marilyn Monroe's problem was that, like Charles Eitel
and Rusty Jethro, she was caught in the corporate
web, in this case Hollywood, and compelled to play
the role it forced upon her, that of vibrant sex goddess. In the process, to recall an image from *The Deer
Park*, the life of the "cave," of the creative mind,
atrophied.

10

○○

Awesome Men:
The Fight and *Genius and Lust*

In his nonfiction Mailer has written so insightfully about the people and events of our national life that now at any new development in our culture, we find ourselves asking the question, "What would Mailer say about it?" We want to know.

However much critics may dispute the merits of his novels, most of them would agree that there is no better journalist in America. *The Fight* would not change their view. The book describes Muhammad Ali's fight with George Foreman in Zaïre (formerly the Congo) to regain the heavyweight championship of the world. Mailer immerses us first in the political and social ambience of the fight. He portrays President Mobutu, iron-willed leader of a new nation, as a mysterious, unapproachable potentate, a man determined to bring the dubious gifts of progress to his people while at the same time making them ever mindful of their—and his—vital connection with the magical energies of tribal traditions. If Ali, messianically proclaiming his Muslim message for the salvation of the black race, is the "Prince of Heaven," Mobutu is the chieftain of fecund darkness.

Kinshasa (formerly Leopoldville) is a city rife with nepotism and poverty. The municipal buildings, aswarm with bureaucratic inefficiency, and the streets, winding through clusters of dusty hovels, are watched

over by Mobutu's soldiers and police. Nonetheless,
there is a growing sense of unity and hope in Zaïre
where black power is a formidable reality. The people
believe in it, more so than ever as Ali comes to town.

The Fight is built around Ali. He lives within it
as a pulsating presence. When he speaks his seriocomic
patter arrays the page:

"If I," said Ali, "give the enemy some of my knowledge,
then maybe he'll have sense to lay back and wait. Of
course I will even convert that to my advantage. I'm
versatile. All the same, the Mummy's best bet is to stand
in the center of the ring and wait for me to come in."
With hardly a pause, he added, "Did you hear that *death*
music he plays? [somber orchestral music piped into the
P. A. system at Foreman's training camp] He *is* the
mummy. And," said Ali chuckling, "I'm going to be the
Mummy's Curse!"

Ali seems a version of Mailer himself, which may
explain Mailer's fascination with him for fifteen years.
If Mailer were less subtle and more loud, he would
resemble Ali more than a little. And if we recall
Mailer's other living hero, Henry Miller, the three
personalities suggest an unmistakable unity. Each man
is the embodiment of loquacious defiance. They are
romantic individualists in an age of growing collectivism, and they both have an inflammable sense of
personal honor. It may not be at all wrong to see them
as sympathetic to the values of the past. How agreeable for Mailer, then, that this book takes him to the
living past, to Africa, where, if technology and trade
are to succeed at all, they must be wedded to tribal
tradition.

Reading *Bantu Philiosophy* by Father Tempels, a
former missionary in the Belgian Congo, Mailer
brightens with the discovery that the philosophy of
African tribesmen is close to his own. A basic premise
guides the book: whereas the American mind sub-

jugates or sublimates primordial instincts, the African
mind allows itself to be informed by them. At the
core of Bantu philosophy is the belief that the human
being is more than the result of environmental and
genetic influences. A man is also the reflection of how
he lived his previous lives. A man is not merely a
socio-biotic entity with his own individual psyche but,
paraphrases Mailer, "a part of the resonance, sympathetic or unsympathetic, of every root or thing (and
witch) about him." To be strong he must catch and
cultivate this "resonance."

Mailer argues that the American black, though
he may not describe his life in this way, lives it in this
way. Bantu philosophy is his heritage, and in its light
Mailer tries to understand Ali. The role of heavyweight
champion of the world has a potent spiritual existence
of its own. Not to seize it constitutes, in Western
terms, an ego loss. Ali is the exemplar of the American
black consciousness that, cut off from African tradition
and transplanted to America, is trying to reconnect
with *kuntu*, the creative, potent flow of forces that
permeate the primeval elements of the universe.

Bantu philosophy is fascinating enough, however,
without Mailer trying to demonstrate it with spiritual
feats of his own. The book becomes silly when he
attempts magically to transfer his courage to Ali by
stepping around the parapet between his hotel balcony
and the adjoining one. A lot of unnecessary spooking
goes on in *The Fight*. He imagines the Ali and
Foreman camps vying for all available stock on a
fluctuating *kuntu* market. Father Tempels would be
bemused.

Mailer's narrative is far more effective when it
excludes the transempirical and attends to the concrete
realities at hand. He visits Foreman's camp; he watches
Ali work out with his sparring partners; he runs with
Ali; he trades quips with promotion men, managers,

and trainers; he is with Ali in his dressing room before
and after the fight; at the Dakar airport on his return
trip to New York, he helps a stewardess assuage a mob
of Africans who, convinced that Ali is aboard the
plane, rush across the runways and insist on seeing
him. Whatever scene Mailer describes, we are right
there with him because his observations wholly delight
us. At fifty-two he has reached that stage where a
rueful, earned wisdom has seasoned his rebel ire and
a sense of common humanity has tempered his
brashness.

Mailer's observations are sly, remarkably perceptive, and always pushing toward those boundaries of
experience beyond which language cannot go. When
he crosses those boundaries, his prose naturally falters.
But such risk taking keeps us reading. His style is
suspenseful. We watch him perform entrechats of
language. Sometimes he slips, as exemplified by his
description of the teeming cricket and locust life of
the African night: "Were insects a part of the cosmos
or the termites of the cosmos?" The more we think
about such a thought the less it means.

But who could do what Mailer does with Ali's
knockout blow to Foreman's head? Invoking metaphors very few writers would ever imagine and none
would dare use, he gives us a description of unforget-
table, unaccountable rightness:

Foreman's arms flew out to the side like a man with a
parachute jumping out of a plane, and in this doubled-over
position he tried to wander out to the center of the ring.
All the while his eyes were on Ali and he looked up with
no anger as if Ali, indeed, was the man he knew best in
the world and would see him on his dying day. Vertigo
took George Foreman and revolved him. Still bowing from
the waist in this uncomprehending position, eyes on
Muhammad Ali all the way, he started to tumble and
topple and fall even as he did not wish to go down. His

mind was held with magnets high as his championship and his body was seeking the ground. He went over like a six-foot sixty-year-old butler who has just heard tragic news, yes, fell over all of a long collapsing two seconds, down came the Champion in sections and Ali revolved with him in a close circle, hand primed to hit him one more time, and never the need, a wholly intimate escort to the floor.

Mailer does here what he does throughout *The Fight*. He harmonizes disparate modes of discourse into one original voice. He chronicles, poeticizes, observes, and analyzes. He works his combinations, much like Ali himself. *The Fight* is the perfect marriage of style and subject. The literature of sport has never seen a better book.

With *Genius and Lust*, an anthology of the works of Henry Miller, Mailer turns full-fledged literary critic. There are about 500 pages by Miller and about 100 pages by Mailer, who early in the book has this to say:

Miller at his best wrote a prose grander than Faulkner's, and wilder—the good reader is revolved in a farrago of light with words heavy as velvet, brilliant as gems, eruptions of thought cover the page. You could be in the vortex of one of Turner's oceanic holocausts when the sun shines in the very center of the storm.

This is impressionistic criticism carried to extravagance, but at bottom, like most of Mailer's assessments in this book, it is quite discerning. The curious thing, however, about this passage is that the honors Mailer ascribes to Miller are the very ones he imagines should be accorded to himself. In 1956 with his columns for *The Village Voice*, Mailer transformed his style, cutting free from the influence of Hemingway, from those direct sentences of studied dispassion, and shifted his allegiance to the stylistic tradition of

Miller. His prose became gusty, dense, exhortative, eloquently cadenced; it purposively flew in the face of "literature." He abandoned Hemingway's clean, well-lighted camp by the side of the river and entered the river itself. "I am the river, he [Miller] is always ready to say, I am the rapids and the placids, I'm the froth and the scum and twigs—what a roar as I go over the falls." When Mailer rhapsodizes over Miller, he is idealizing himself.

Genius and Lust can be read not only as its subtitle states, as "a journey through the major writings of Henry Miller," but as an overview of Norman Mailer the writer, for Mailer shares practically the same strengths and defects as Miller. Yet it should be established at the outset that in some significant respects these two men can hardly be called literary brothers or, as a proper regard for time would dictate, father and son (Miller is 86 and Mailer 55). Miller is the last of the buoyant anarchists, a novelist of hearty diabolisms who has always written as he pleased, remaining all but deaf to the world's censure. Trophies, adversative or admiring critics, and fat royalties have been to him very much beside the point. Mailer, on the other hand, has been working since the mid 1950s at the impossible task of disturbing people and then coaxing them to adore him. He is a creature of topicalities, consistently choosing as his subject matter the events, the celebrities, the issues that the nation itself, for reasons he is always trying to divine, has chosen. It is hard to imagine Miller, an unregenerate bohemian sequestered from the clamorous world in his hermitage at Big Sur, appearing on TV, negotiating for movie rights, making big-time deals with publishers, and meeting deadlines.

Still, the arresting fact remains that the work of Miller and Mailer coalesce at some very important points. If it has been Miller's Promethean aim, as

Mailer says, to "alter the nerves and marrow of a
nation," it has been Mailer's to effect "a revolution in
the consciousness of our time," as he states in *Advertisements for Myself*. The quiet old satyr of California
would probably deem Mailer's estimation of his
novelistic purpose a bit inflated. And it *is* inflated if
we view Miller's work as a whole. But his early novels
—*Tropic of Cancer, Black Spring, Tropic of Capricorn*
(excerpts from which compose over half this book)—
did very much intend to drastically reshape the mind
of man, and in so doing necessarily set out to remake
literature by destroying it. Almost immediately in
Tropic of Cancer Miller says: "This then? This is not
a book. This is libel, slander, defamation of character.
This is not a book, in the ordinary sense of the word.
No, this is a prolonged insult, a gob of spit in the face
of Art, a kick in the pants to God, Man, Destiny, Time,
Love, Beauty . . . what you will." In his own defiant
idiom, Mailer made a similar avowal in *Advertisements
for Myself* when he wrote that his artistic intention
was to "mate the absurd with the apocalyptic," to
merge "the extreme, the obscene and the unsayable,"
"to attempt an entrance into the mysteries of murder,
suicide, incest, orgy, orgasm, and Time."

Miller and Mailer are inveterate renegades who
share a common enemy. The great noise, let us call it,
that seems to Mailer to be getting louder and louder
with every passing year—the noise of government,
technology, advertising, and of every clamorous need
of the bourgeois for regulation, conformity, and
security. Such a cultural condition militates against the
American artist—and, by extension, the thinking,
imaginative man—and turns him into a rebel or a
victim.

Mailer shares obsessions with Miller as well as
defiances. Both show a symbolic connection between
sexual transgression and moral freedom. Their books

are testimonies to the proposition that a life of sexual
vagabondage can be as worthwhile and as honest as
many another life. When Miller was writing in those
four decades before the 1970s, he did not have to
justify this proposition to women. In 1971, with *The
Prisoner of Sex*, Mailer did and enlisted Miller to run
interference for him against the attacking new feminists. If Miller degrades women in bed and uses them
as carnal fodder, Mailer wrote in that book, it is
because he is in awe of their life-bearing powers, their
mysterious alliance with the gestating energies of the
cosmos, and so he feels he must, perhaps out of some
kind of deeply envious wonder, cut them down, debase
them. This is as stupendous a piece of illogic as
Mailer has ever committed. In *Genius and Lust* he
commits it again when he says that Miller's "dread"
of women's intimate closeness to the source of all
creation makes him "revile them, humiliate them . . .
do everything to reduce them so that he might dare
to enter them and take pleasure of them." Nonetheless,
Mailer's claim for Miller's greatness cannot be denied:
he was the first writer to break down the inhibiting
walls of American fiction and introduce the sex act as
a subject for serious novelistic treatment.

When it comes time for Mailer to discuss Miller's
later and lesser works and to include excerpts from
them (*The Rosy Crucifixion, The Air-Conditioned
Nightmare, Sunday after the War, Big Sur*), he admits
to Miller's defects without being too particular to name
them. He says only that "There is not one Henry Miller
but twenty, and fifteen of those authors are very good."
His reticence about the weaknesses of Miller's writing
may spring from the possible fact that in elucidating
the master, the pupil finds himself looking into a mirror
which reflects his own blemishes. He is not too eager
to make a case of them. Yet it remains that both
writers lapse on occasion into what one might call

"word drunkenness"—amorphous, onrushing displays of private philosophy and phantasmagoria. And they tend at times to substitute discourse for drama, to tell when they should be showing.

But such criticism of writers the like of these serves only to show the obverse side of their greatness. At their best they possess the kind of rebelliousness that at once outrages and fascinates. Their work begins in defiance but ends in discovery. Their backs are up, but they seem all the while to be dancing. More significantly for Mailer, however, there is a certain strategy for survival expressed in *Tropic of Cancer* that he has taken as a major lesson to be learned and incorporated into his own work. Henry Miller, down and out on the foul streets of Paris, stays alive and happy by dissolving his ego in identification with the chaos around it. It is a perilous strategy, but one that has the potential of winning for him the opportunity he desires as an artist, the opportunity to deeply know the world. He takes in and controls, by the power of the creative imagination, forces in the world that would otherwise destroy him. Mailer dramatizes this maneuver in his characterization of Stephen Rojack in *An American Dream* and with D. J. Jethro in *Why Are We in Vietnam?* "Man learns more about the nature of water . . . if he comes close to drowning," Mailer once said in an interview.[1] This statement lies as close to the heart of his philosophy as any statement he has ever uttered. We can hear the voice of Miller behind it. If the task Mailer set himself in *Genius and Lust* was to gain a wider public prominence for the work of Henry Miller, it was also to pay back a long outstanding debt.

11

○ ○

Conclusion:
The Essential Conflict

The fiction of Norman Mailer up to and including *The Deer Park* concerns man trying to achieve a self-fulfilling autonomy that takes into realistic account the social and biological forces of life and guards against the delusive security of conventional moralities. The early fiction asks: what is the world that man may understand it? But when the mixed reception of *The Deer Park* turned Mailer into an impassioned outlaw, his fiction underwent a radical change. The emphasis shifted. A new question was asked: what is man that the world may understand him? In the early fiction, reality acted upon consciousness. In the later fiction, consciousness acts upon reality, or rather transforms it through the egocentric imagination. The direction of Mailer's fiction, then, has been from the mimetic to the expressive, from a world described to a world envisioned.

There were artistic penalties to pay. *An American Dream* and *Why Are We in Vietnam?*, for all their power, verged on solipsism. A self bent on transcending the world's necessities risks distorting them in the heat of an all too personalized vision. The distinctive character of Mailer's non-fiction, *The Armies of the Night* and *Miami and the Siege of Chicago*, is that the exigencies of social and political fact subdue the extravagance of his imagination.

History chastened Mailer and provided occasion for him to make of his art the perfect fusion of abstraction and objectification, romance and realism. Expressiveness and mimesis became reconciled at last.

Whatever formal or artistic differences we find among Mailer's works, we should not imagine a thematic difference when, in fact, none exists. An essential conflict undergirds all Mailer's books and makes them indivisible: the conflict between will and external power.

The real moral power of Mailer's writing derives from his depiction of human will and human imagination battling against the forces of constraint. The only thing that operates for good in Mailer's world is the individual fighting alone against the institutional powers that be. No collective effort, no group or social program, no matter how intent on justice, can win Mailer's serious allegiance because man in the aggregate, he believes, becomes less than man; he loses his honor, his dignity, his selfhood. Sam Croft against Mount Anaka, Sergius O'Shaugnessy against Hollywood, Stephen Rojack against Barney Oswald Kelly, D. J. Jethro against the corporation, Norman Mailer against the Pentagon—it is always one man struggling against a mighty power intent on possessing his soul.

But the struggle often turns out to be not as valiant as all that. In Mailer's world, to test oneself against any implacable power is to be caught visibly in contradictions: to attempt seriousness and fall into clownishness; to become doctrinaire in defying the doctrinal; to skirt a ledge between heroism and absurdity; to shift precariously between clarity and turgidity, reason and dream, generosity and self-obsession, libertarianism and autocracy; to be Prometheus with the compulsions of Icarus.

Yet Mailer does not try to neutralize any of these polarities in himself. He refuses to put together a harmonious personality because he suspects that consistency is only another name for inertia. For Mailer, life as it is lived in the modern world is degraded. His basic view has always been that the institutions of society—government, business, marriage, church, the military—are deadening and want man to adopt death as life. To resist in order to make possible that awakening that literature attempts is Mailer's reason for being.

And more. A spiritual fervor kindles the heart of Mailer's rebellion; for ultimately it is not what men make or do that evokes his opposition, but the very terms of human mortality itself. He insists on believing that man is supernatural, not natural. His struggle, then, has been mythic, epical. On the basis of *Advertisements for Myself, An American Dream, Why Are We in Vietnam?, The Armies of the Night*, and *Miami and the Siege of Chicago*, a fair claim can be made: the magnitude of Mailer's imagination and his extraordinary powers of expressiveness have restored to English literature the fertile, energetic grandeur it has seldom known since the seventeenth century.

Notes

1. Biography

1. Anthony Burgess, "The Novel in America," *Times Literary Supplement*, 4 Aug. 1972, p. 916.
2. Joe Flaherty, *Managing Mailer* (New York: Coward-McCann, 1970), p. 118.
3. Anna Rothe and Constance Ellis, eds., *Current Biography, 1948* (New York: H. W. Wilson, 1949), p. 408.
4. Raymond A. Sokolov, "Flying High with Mailer," *Newsweek*, 9 Dec. 1968, p. 86.
5. Norman Mailer, *Advertisements for Myself* (New York: Putnam's, 1966), p. 65.
6. Ibid.
7. Stanley J. Kunitz and Vineta Colby, eds., *Twentieth Century Authors* (New York: H. W. Wilson, 1955), p. 628.
8. *Current Biography, 1948*, p. 409.
9. Mailer, *Advertisements for Myself*, p. 25.
10. "The Talk of the Town," *The New Yorker*, 25 Oct. 1948, p. 25.
11. Mailer, *Advertisements for Myself*, p. 86.
12. Brock Brower, "Always the Challenger," *Life*, 24 Sept. 1965, p. 111.
13. Ibid., p. 112.
14. "The Talk of the Town," *The New Yorker*, 25 Oct. 1948, p. 25.
15. Norman Mailer, *Genius and Lust: A Journey Through*

the Major Writings of Henry Miller (New York: Grove Press, 1976), p. 93.

16. Stan Isaacs, "Mailer, the Ezzard Charles of Literature," *International Herald Tribune*, 10 Oct. 1975, p. 14.
17. "Norman Mailer on Women, Love, Sex, Politics, and All That!" *Cosmopolitan*, May 1976, p. 184.
18. Mark Goodman, "Bio," *People*, 10 Nov. 1975, p. 50.
19. Mailer, *Advertisements for Myself*, p. 439.

2. THWARTED WILL: *The Naked and the Dead*

1. This paragraph is based on Albert Camus's discussion of rebellion and resentment in *The Rebel: An Essay on Man in Revolt* (New York: Random House, 1956), p. 17.
2. Kenneth Clark, *Civilisation* (New York: Harper & Row, 1970), p. 238.

4. THE ARTIST'S PLIGHT: *The Deer Park*

1. Richard Foster, *Norman Mailer*, Univ. of Minnesota Pamphlets on American Writers, No. 73 (Minneapolis: Univ. of Minnesota Press, 1968), p. 17.

5. THE WRITER AS OUTLAW: *Advertisements for Myself*

1. Roy Harvey Pearce, *The Continuity of American Poetry* (Princeton, New Jersey: Princeton Univ. Press, 1967), p. 276.

6. THE NEW HERO: *An American Dream*

1. Laura Adams, "Existential Aesthetics: An Interview with Norman Mailer," *Partisan Review* (July 1975), 199.

2. Leo Bersani, "The Interpretation of Dreams," *Norman Mailer: A Collection of Critical Essays*, ed. Leo Braudy (Englewood Cliffs, New Jersey: Prentice-Hall, 1972), p. 178.

3. Richard Poirier, "Morbid-mindedness," *Norman Mailer: The Man and His Work*, ed. Robert F. Lucid (Boston: Little Brown, 1971), p. 170.

4. See Robert Solotaroff, *Down Mailer's Way*, p. 175 and Stanley Edgar Hyman, "Norman Mailer's Yummy Rump," *Norman Mailer: A Collection of Critical Essays*, ed. Leo Braudy, pp. 105–6.

5. Foster, *Norman Mailer*, p. 19.

7. AN ALASKAN ODYSSEY: *Why Are We in Vietnam?*

1. John Aldridge, "From Vietnam to Obscenity," *Norman Mailer: The Man and His Work*, ed. Robert F. Lucid, p. 189.

2. Ibid., pp. 189–90.

3. William Burroughs, *Naked Lunch* (New York: Grove Press, 1959), p. 11.

4. Richard Chase, *The American Novel and Its Tradition* (Garden City, New York: Doubleday, 1957), p. 7.

8. HISTORY INTO ART: *The Armies of the Night, Miami and the Siege of Chicago,* and *Of a Fire on the Moon*

1. Tom Wolfe, *The New Journalism* (New York: Harper & Row, 1973), p. 34.

2. Melvin Maddocks, "Norm's Ego Is Working Overtime for YOU," *Life*, 10 May 1968, p. 8.

9. AWESOME WOMEN:
The Prisoner of Sex and *Marilyn*

1. Brigid Brophy, *"The Prisoner of Sex," The New York Times Book Review*, 23 May 1971, p. 16.

2. Joyce Carol Oates, "Out of the Machine," *Atlantic*, July 1971, pp. 44–45.

10. AWESOME MEN: *The Fight* and *Genius and Lust*

1. Raymond A. Sokolov, "Flying High with Mailer," *Newsweek*, 9 Dec. 1968, p. 87.

Bibliography

I. BOOKS BY NORMAN MAILER

The Naked and the Dead. New York: Rinehart, 1948.

Barbary Shore. New York: Rinehart, 1951.

The Deer Park. New York: Putnam's, 1955.

The White Negro: Superficial Reflections on the Hipster. San Francisco: City Lights, 1958.

Advertisements for Myself. New York: Putnam's, 1959.

Deaths for the Ladies (and Other Disasters). New York: Putnam's, 1962.

The Presidential Papers. New York: Putnam's, 1963.

An American Dream. New York: Dial, 1965.

Cannibals and Christians. New York: Dial, 1966.

The Bullfight: A Photographic Narrative with Text by Norman Mailer. New York: C. B. S. Legacy Collection Book, distributed by the Macmillan Company, 1967.

The Deer Park: A Play. New York: Dial, 1967.

The Short Fiction of Norman Mailer. New York: Dell, 1967.

Why Are We in Vietnam? New York: Putnam's, 1967.

The Idol and the Octopus: Political Writings by Norman Mailer on the Kennedy and Johnson Administrations. New York: Dell, 1968.

The Armies of the Night: History as a Novel/The Novel as History. New York: New American Library, 1968.

Miami and the Siege of Chicago: An Informal History of the Republican and Democratic Conventions of 1968. New York: New American Library, 1968.

Of a Fire on the Moon. Boston: Little, Brown, 1971.

The Prisoner of Sex. Boston: Little, Brown, 1971.

On the Fight of the Century: King of the Hill. New York: New American Library, 1971.

Maidstone: A Mystery. New York: New American Library, 1971.

Existential Errands. Boston: Little, Brown, 1972.

St. George and the Godfather. New York: New American Library, 1972.

Marilyn: A Biography. New York: Grosset & Dunlap, 1973.

The Faith of Graffiti. New York: Praeger, 1974. Photographs by Mervyn Kurlansky and Jon Naar. Text by Norman Mailer.

The Fight. Boston: Little, Brown, 1975.

Genius and Lust: A Journey Through the Major Writings of Henry Miller. New York: Grove Press, 1976.

Some Honorable Men: Political Conventions 1960–1972. Boston: Little, Brown, 1976.

II. BOOKS ABOUT NORMAN MAILER

Adams, Laura. *A Bibliography of Norman Mailer*. Metuchen, New Jersey: Scarecrow, 1974.

—————. *Existential Battles: The Growth of Norman Mailer*. Athens, Ohio: Ohio Univ. Press, 1976.

—————, ed. *Will the Real Norman Mailer Please Stand Up?* Port Washington, New York: Kennikat, 1973.

Braudy, Leo, ed. *Norman Mailer: A Collection of Critical Essays*. Englewood Cliffs, New Jersey: Prentice-Hall, 1972.

Flaherty, Joe. *Managing Mailer*. New York: Coward-McCann, 1970.

Foster, Richard. *Norman Mailer*. Minneapolis: Univ. of Minnesota Pamphlets on American Writers, No. 73, 1968.

Gutman, Stanley T. *Mankind in Barbary: The Individual and Society in the Novels of Norman Mailer*. Hanover, New Hampshire: University Press of New England, 1975.

Kaufmann, Donald L. *Norman Mailer: The Countdown*

(The First Twenty Years). Carbondale, Illinois: Univ. of Southern Illinois Press, 1969.

Leeds, Barry H. *The Structured Vision of Norman Mailer*. New York: New York Univ. Press, 1969.

Lucid, Robert F., ed. *Norman Mailer: The Man and His Work*. Boston: Little, Brown, 1971.

Manso, Peter, ed. *Running Against the Machine: The Mailer-Breslin Campaign*. Garden City, New York: Doubleday, 1969.

Middlebrook, Jonathan. *Mailer and the Times of His Time*. San Francisco: Bay Books, 1976.

Poirier, Richard. *Norman Mailer*. New York: Viking, 1972.

Radford, Jean. *Norman Mailer: A Critical Study*. New York: Harper & Row, 1975.

Solotaroff, Robert. *Down Mailer's Way*. Urbana, Illinois: Univ. of Illinois Press, 1974.

Weatherby, W. S. *Squaring Off: Mailer vs. Baldwin*. New York: Mason/Charter, 1977.

Index

WASPs, views on, 26, 77, 79,
    99–100, 104
"White Negro, The," 49, 57,
    59–60, 68, 78, 114
Whitman, Walt, 53, 89, 101
Why Are We in Vietnam?, 12,
    75–84, 87, 91, 118, 129,
    131, 133

Wolf, Daniel, 9–10
Wolfe, Thomas, 5, 7
Wolfe, Tom, 87
Woolf, Virginia, 61

Young Lions, The (Shaw), 28

Zolotow, Maurice, 116

MODERN LITERATURE MONOGRAPHS

In the same series (continued from page ii)